ROB RENFROE

# THE TROUBLE

## *with the*

# TRUTH

## BALANCING
## TRUTH AND GRACE

Nashville
Abingdon Press

THE TROUBLE WITH THE TRUTH

*Copyright © 2014 Abingdon Press*

All rights reserved.

No part of this work may be reproduced or transmitted in any form or by any means, electronic or mechanical, including photocopying and recording, or by any information storage or retrieval system, except as may be expressly permitted by the 1976 Copyright Act or in writing from the publisher. Requests for permission can be addressed to Permissions, The United Methodist Publishing House, P.O. Box 801, 201 Eighth Avenue South, Nashville, TN 37202-0801, or e-mailed to permissions@umpublishing.org.

*This book is printed on acid-free paper.*

ISBN 978-1-4267-8619-8

All Scripture quotations, unless otherwise indicated, are taken from the Holy Bible, New International Version®, NIV®. Copyright © 1973, 1978, 1984, 2011 by Biblica, Inc.™ Used by permission of Zondervan. All rights reserved worldwide. www.zondervan.com. The "NIV" and "New International Version" are trademarks registered in the United States Patent and Trademark Office by Biblica, Inc.™

Scripture quotations marked CEB are from the Common English Bible. Copyright © 2011 by the Common English Bible. All rights reserved. Used by permission. www.CommonEnglishBible.com.

Scripture quotations marked "NKJV™" are taken from the New King James Version®. Copyright © 1982 by Thomas Nelson, Inc. Used by permission. All rights reserved.

Scripture quotations marked NRSV are taken from the New Revised Standard Version of the Bible, copyright 1989, Division of Christian Education of the National Council of the Churches of Christ in the United States of America. Used by permission. All rights reserved.

Scripture quotations marked (ESV) are from The Holy Bible, English Standard Version® (ESV®), copyright © 2001 by Crossway, a publishing ministry of Good News Publishers. Used by permission. All rights reserved.

14 15 16 17 18 19 20 21 22 23—10 9 8 7 6 5 4 3 2
MANUFACTURED IN THE UNITED STATES OF AMERICA

*To Eddie Wills, whose life of grace and truth
caused me to fall in love with Jesus.*

# Contents

# Introduction

As we make our way into the twenty-first century, scientific and technological advancements are taking place at an incredible rate. As a race, we are rightfully proud and amazed at our progress in understanding the physical universe that is our home. But in terms of understanding the truth about ourselves, we in the West have never been as confused as we are now. When we try to answer many of life's most important questions— questions such as what makes us human, what defines a life well lived, are there moral truths that apply to all of us and, if so, what are they—there is no consensus whatsoever.

We are not only uncertain about what is true about ourselves. We, as a culture, no longer even agree where to look for answers. Does science tell us all we need to know about ourselves and how to live well, or are the answers we seek not to be found "out there" but inside ourselves as we listen to the inherent wisdom that resides within our hearts? Is it possible that the knowledge we crave can be found in ancient texts written by sages and prophets who were guided by divine inspiration, or will the universe gladly unveil itself and our place in it if we learn to look past the physical and open our spirits to what is eternal?

Which of these paths is most likely to lead us to what is most true about ourselves as human beings? The truth is, we don't know. Or maybe it's better to say, we can't agree. There is no consensus in Western culture about life's most important truths or even how to determine which of the many possibilities is most likely to be correct.

Talk show hosts and pundits of all persuasions talk about "culture wars." But there's something much deeper and even more troubling that is occurring. Beneath our differences about the values that should define our culture is a real disagreement about what is true. Our values, both as individuals and as a culture, are founded on what we believe is morally right and spiritually true. Thus, the "culture wars" are symptoms of a deeper problem: there is trouble with the truth. And as long as there is trouble with the truth, there will be trouble with us.

What we believe to be true matters because truth is how we answer life's big questions. Who are we as human beings? What is the purpose of life? How should we as individuals conduct our lives and treat each other? How do we live together as a community of diverse people? Is there a God? And if so, what, if anything, does our Creator expect of us?

The reason our culture is so divided and so many people are full of anger and vitriol as they discuss our differences is because our disagreement goes much deeper than whether we should say "Merry Christmas" or "Happy Holidays." It's more basic than whether marijuana should be legalized for recreational use or banned completely. It's even more foundational than whether abortion is a woman's right to control her body or the taking of innocent life. It is a disagreement about what is true spiritually and morally.

As we will see, the cultural divide regarding truth is not only wider than ever before; it's different than it has ever been. Until the middle part of the twentieth century, even if we in the West disagreed about the truth, the general belief was that "the truth is out there"[1] somewhere and is true for all of us. But since that time, a postmodern understanding of reality has come to shape how we think about truth. At the heart of postmodernism—the predominant cultural worldview of our time, which we will explore in this book—is the belief that truth is not singular. In other words, there are no universal spiritual or moral truths that apply to all of us. There are only personal truths, truths that we as individuals find to work for us, and none of these truths is any better or more real than any other.

As a result of postmodernism, our cultural conversation concerning values has become even more difficult. Some of us believe there are overarching spiritual truths and moral obligations that are as valid today as they ever have been. And we want to know what those truths are and how we can live accordingly. But those with a postmodern mind—whether they have fully subscribed to postmodern ideas or have been subtly and unknowingly influenced by them—think differently. Believing there are no universal truths, they do not simply find those of us who do to be wrong. Many postmoderns find us to be offensive. And their question is, "Who do you think you are to claim that you have the truth?"

This book is for classical Christians—believers who hold to the traditional beliefs of the Christian faith—who, as I do, sense that our culture is in trouble. Though all of us may not know how to put it into words, we sense that many of the problems in our culture are rooted in the fact that there is trouble with the truth as we make our way into the twenty-first century. We understand that the trouble is not just "out there in the culture"; it's also in the church. We grieve that the divide within the church is just as emotionally charged as it is in the culture— often over the same issues. At a time when our broken, lost world desperately needs the church of Jesus Christ to speak clearly with a unified voice words of healing and truth, the church seems as confused as the culture.

When the president of a mainline denominational seminary, who has certainly read Jesus' final command in Matthew 28:19 that we are to "make disciples of all nations," states publicly that Christians who feel they need to evangelize persons of other faiths have a wrong view of what it means to follow Jesus, there's trouble with the truth.

When Jesus claimed to be "the way and the truth and the life" (John 14:6) but now it is common for mainline pastors and parishioners to state, "Well, Jesus is my way, but who am I to say there aren't other ways for other people," there's trouble with the truth.

When the apostles were persecuted and put to death because they refused to deny the earliest Christian affirmation of faith "Jesus Christ is Lord"—a bold and dangerous assertion that Jesus alone was absolutely unique and authoritative and, in fact, God in the flesh—but today in the West those who claim the name of Christ often say "all the world's great religions teach the same thing," there's trouble with the truth.

And when a highly respected pastor who taught ethics in one of the world's great medical centers says (as he did to me) that the church created the Scriptures and so we can re-create the Scriptures, there's trouble with the truth.

The church has always been influenced by its culture. Sadly, throughout history the church has at times become worldly and corrupt and has had to be reformed and renewed. But something different and more dangerous is occurring in our time. The church and too many of its leaders are adopting the culture's view of truth—a philosophy that makes morality nothing more than a personal preference and the Christian faith nothing more than one of many options that may work for you or, if not, that may be discarded in favor of some other "truth" that is more to your liking. In this book we will look together at the truth—why it's in trouble, what the culture tells us about it, and why the church is so confused about it. My hope is that you will come to be certain that you can be a person of both grace and truth. I hope you will be more convinced than ever that the gospel of Jesus Christ is a true and sure foundation for your life and for the lives of others. And I hope you will know that you can hold onto the truth with all your might and at the same time reach out an open hand to persons who disagree with you. Not only can we do this, but we must because we follow the One who did.

This leads me to a final word. Whenever we discuss the God of the universe and the truth he has revealed, we must do so with great humility. God is not only larger than we can imagine; he is different than we are. The biblical word is *holy*. He transcends what we are capable of comprehending. We may speak about God's being and will only because in his grace he has condescended to make himself known to us.

Simply because I believe in absolute truths does not mean that I believe I have the truth absolutely. Life is a journey for all of us—a journey of learning and growing—and none of us has yet arrived, certainly not myself. I feel certain that all of us who seek to know and do God's will, regardless of theology, share the same humility of knowing that we are limited creatures trying to understand and be faithful to a God whose wisdom, power, and grace are much greater than we will ever fully comprehend.

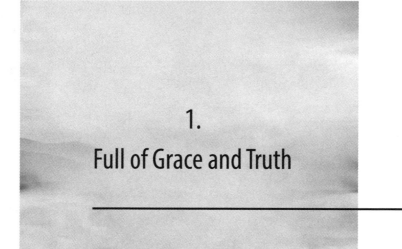

# 1.
# Full of Grace and Truth

# 1.
# Full of Grace and Truth

At the heart of the universe, there is a heart of grace. It's the heart of one Jesus described as a loving Father, one who finds joy in bringing good gifts into the lives of his children. It's the heart of a shepherd who discovers that one of his sheep is missing, so he leaves the ninety-nine to find the one that's lost. It's the breaking heart of one who is looking a long way off for a rebellious, wandering son and who runs to embrace his retuning child, kiss his face, and forgive his transgressions.

This heart of grace is also a heart of truth. It is a heart that is offended by lies and deception and hypocrisy. This heart belongs to a God who tells us that the truth will set us free and warns us about teachers who tell people what they want to hear and are willing to remove the "offense" of the gospel when contending for the faith proves unpopular or costly. At the heart of the universe there is truth as eternal and as unchanging as the God who has revealed it.

At the heart of the universe, there is a heart of compassion—a compassion so great that God could not turn his back on those who turned their backs on him; a compassion so great that God himself came into our world in the person of Jesus to seek and save the lost, knowing that if he did so, he would be scorned and mistreated and ultimately nailed to a cross.

This heart of compassion is also a heart of righteousness. It is the heart of one who delights in all that is good and who is grieved by all that is evil. It's the heart of a God who sent prophets to demand that his people be pure in heart and just in their actions, and that they repent of their sins.

At the heart of the universe, there is a heart of love. Nothing is more real—not the earth beneath our feet, not the pain we suffer, not the sins we commit. Before any physical realities came into existence, there was love. And when the earth and our pain and our sins are no more, love will remain.

This heart of love is also a heart of holiness. It is a heart that cannot be neutral about evil without denying its very nature. It is the heart of a God who cannot ignore the wrongs done by his creatures because evil not only does harm to those who are wronged but also mars his image in the one who does the wrong.

When the Father sent the Son into the world that we might be saved, he came with grace and truth, compassion and righteousness, love and holiness. Without grace and truth together, we don't have the God of the Bible. Without compassion and righteousness together, we don't have Jesus of the Gospels. Without love and holiness together, we don't have the good news. The Christian faith is not one instead of the other or one more than the other but both together in equal measure, because this is the nature of our God.

## The Perfect Combination

The Gospel of John begins with a picture of God entering our world and making himself known in the person of Jesus. John's description of "The Beautiful One" opens with a sentence that may be at the same time one of the simplest and most profound ever written. When I was a sophomore at Rice University,

John 1:1 was the first sentence we read and translated in Greek 101. Even then I was struck by the elegance and power of the Greek, which is translated "In the beginning was the Word, and the Word was with God, and the Word was God."

"The Word," of course, is Jesus, and John tells us more about Jesus' coming into the world later in his prologue: "The Word became flesh and made his dwelling among us. We have seen his glory, the glory of the one and only Son, who came from the Father, full of grace and truth" (John 1:14). When John describes the beautiful life of Jesus, he says that Jesus came with both grace and truth.

Grace is compassion for people. Grace is being better to people than their actions deserve. It's trying to understand their struggles, caring for their needs, and sharing their burdens. We see this grace in the ministry of Jesus over and over again throughout the Gospels.

Jesus also came with a passion for truth. He spoke the words that people needed to hear even if they didn't want to hear them. He was faithful to his principles even when doing so angered the authorities. He refused to compromise his message even when he knew that he would lose followers as a result— even when he suspected that if he continued to proclaim the truth he would be nailed to a cross. Jesus was as committed to the truth as he was to grace.

Grace and truth—we see them both in the most beautiful and powerful life ever lived. I believe that one reason Jesus dramatically impacted the lives of so many in his day was that he perfectly combined compassion for people with passion for truth, and that's one reason why his words and life still have the power to transform people two thousand years later. I am convinced that if we, as individuals and as God's people together, are to be instruments of real influence and transformation in our time, then we will have to learn how to combine grace and truth in the same way that Jesus did.

## A Balancing Act

Balancing grace and truth isn't easy. It's like walking a tightrope, holding onto a long pole to help you keep your balance.

Many of us watched aerialist Nik Wallenda walk across the Little Colorado River Gorge near the Grand Canyon on June 23, 2013. Fifteen hundred feet above the canyon floor, he walked on a tightrope for a quarter of a mile, trying to keep his balance as the wind blew at speeds of thirty miles an hour. It was excruciating just watching him make the twenty-two-minute journey. If his pole tipped too much one way or the other, he would fall off the wire and plunge to his death.[1]

Trying to live and minister the way Jesus did is something of a high wire act, too. To keep our balance, we hold onto the gospel like an aerialist holding onto a balance pole. On the one side there is grace. On the other is truth. Let the pole tip too much one way or the other, and we'll lose our balance. Lean either way too strongly, and we'll fall off. It's only as we hold the pole in balance that we can walk the way that Jesus walked, live the way that he lived, and impact our world in a way that is truly transformative.

None of us does this balancing act perfectly. We are all influenced by a myriad of factors that affect how we combine compassion for people with passion for truth. Usually we aren't even aware of how they shape our ideas about grace and truth.

*Cultural Influences*

Many of the factors that influence how we think about living a balanced life of grace and truth stem from our culture. Some

To keep our balance, we hold onto the
gospel like an aerialist holding onto a
balance pole. On the one side there
is grace. On the other is truth. . . .
It's only as we hold the pole in
balance that we can walk
the way that Jesus walked.

cultures seem to value compassion more than truth, and others seem to value truth more than compassion. Without question, our Western culture today values compassion—which often is wrongly defined as words or actions that make someone feel good—much more than it does truth.

We care so much about the feelings of others that often we don't keep score at children's sporting events because we think that the truth about who won or lost a game might damage their fragile self-images. With adults, it's not much different. If you speak words that someone else finds offensive, the assumption is often that you have stepped over some boundary of political correctness. The assumption is rarely that the other person may have misunderstood your intent or is being too sensitive. If you believe that you're right and others are wrong in matters of spirituality and morality, you'll probably be labeled "intolerant." If you claim to know "the truth" and it contradicts what others believe, our society generally says that you are judgmental, you don't appreciate diversity, and your views are hurtful and harmful. Many of our most popular television shows, movies, and newspapers, as well as websites and college courses devoted to cultural events, perpetuate the message that anyone who claims to have "the truth" is naïve and bigoted.

The winds of our culture influence us to lean toward compassion rather than truth. The problem is not emphasizing compassion; it's forgetting that in order to be like Jesus, we must hold onto truth just as tightly.

## The Influence of the Church

The church also plays a significant role in influencing our beliefs about grace and truth. If you attended church when you were young, that church helped to form you and your thinking, including your beliefs about grace and truth. And if you are attending a church now, that church is, to some degree, shaping your beliefs about how you should balance compassion for people with passion for truth.

Some churches place a high value on knowing, understanding, and teaching truth. Nothing wrong with that. The problem comes when the necessary balance of grace is missing. When a church spends more time teaching its members what they should believe about secondary doctrines such as the tribulation or predestination than it spends telling them about Jesus' heart for the poor, it's not a healthy church. When the litmus test for being a good member is agreeing with a church's leadership on relatively minor matters of doctrine instead of loving God and neighbor, chances are it's not transforming its members into people who live and minister as Jesus did.

Other churches seem not to be as concerned about what their members believe. They seem to devalue the distinctive truth claims of the Christian faith and instead stress being a caring and open person who doesn't judge others. And who can fault a church that tells its people to love God and love others? But there's a problem when the necessary balance of truth is missing. Jesus came with grace and truth, yet some of his followers care much less about truth than grace. Churches that emphasize grace are doing a good thing—unless they downplay the importance of the truth, which many do.

I once spoke to a group of pastors, and after I finished a young man in his early twenties approached me. He said that he was the pastor of three small churches in a rural area of Tennessee. He told me, "They're very different." I thought to myself, *How can three small country churches only a few miles from each other be "very different"?* So, I asked, "How so?"

He replied, "One wants me to yell at them and tell them how bad they are. One wants me to yell and tell them how bad other people are. And the other one doesn't want me to yell, and they don't think anybody is bad."

I had to laugh. They were different. And none of them got it right. We need grace and truth. Teaching and preaching truth is good, but it becomes a problem when we emphasize our sins more than we do God's grace. And opening our arms to welcome and accept everyone sure sounds like Jesus, unless it also means we can't say, "This is good and that is bad; this is right and that is wrong; this is truth and that is not."

Maybe your congregation is getting it just right. But most churches lean one way or the other. Does your congregation worry more about "right doctrine" than it does about welcoming the last, the least, and the lost who may not be living "the right way"? Or in the name of being accepting, is your church conveying that it doesn't matter what you believe as long as you believe something? The apostles were not martyred for telling people to believe "something." They were put to death because they would not stop preaching the uniqueness of the Christian faith. Whether you realize it or not, your church experience is influencing you in one direction more than the other—and that experience is significantly shaped by your pastor and church leaders and teachers.

I am a preacher, and I know plenty of other preachers; and trust me, very few of us get it just right when it comes to balancing grace and truth. Like other Christians, we too tend to lean more one way than the other—more toward grace or more toward truth. Some pastors tend to emphasize grace. Yet for some of these pastors, their primary goal on Sunday morning seems to be for you to leave church feeling good. They want you to leave worship feeling great about God, the church, and yourself. They want you to head out into the world humming that James Brown favorite, "I f-e-e-e-l good." And there are pastors who emphasize "the truth." Regrettably, some of these pastors do so in a rather warped way, thinking that they don't deserve a paycheck for the week if they can't make you slink out of church feeling worse about yourself than when you first slunk into church.

How you came to faith in Christ also tends to determine whether you place more value on compassion for people or the importance of truth. If you came to Christ because of the warmth, acceptance, and love of a church or a particular person, then you're more likely to believe that this is how people should come to Christ and, consequently, to emphasize grace. If your journey to faith involved a long, intellectual search for satisfying answers to deep questions, then you're more likely to believe that this is how people should come to Christ and, consequently, to stress truth when sharing Christ with others.

With all of these influences, each of us tends to lean more one way than the other. If we will take an honest look at ourselves, most of us will see that we tend to be more of a "gracer" or a "truther."

Gracers want everyone to know how much they're loved and accepted. Gracers really do believe that if people only knew how much God cares for them, then they could accept themselves, their lives would change, and they would be happy. It's natural for gracers to reach out, throw their arms around others, and hope that through their love lost souls will experience God's loving embrace.

Truthers come at it differently. Truthers will tell you that there are many people who know they are loved and who feel good about themselves but still are wandering away from God. They will tell you that there's right and there's wrong. There are truths and principles that God has written into the fabric of the universe, such as humility, honesty, generosity, faithfulness, and self-denial, and people need to live accordingly if they are

Our culture, our own experiences,
and too often the church can set
us up to think about grace and truth
as an "either-or" choice when
what we see consistently in the
life of Jesus is "both grace and truth,"
not one instead of the other or
one more than the other but
both together in equal measure.

going to be right with themselves and right with God. After all, Jesus said, "The truth will set you free" (John 8:32).

So, which are you? Do you find yourself more naturally inclined toward grace or toward truth? Personally, it's my nature to want to be the grace guy, not the truth guy. I love saying and doing what makes people feel loved and affirmed. And I hate it when I think that my words have caused someone discomfort or pain—even if they needed to be said. But I know that I must be as passionate about the truth as I am about grace, because Jesus was. Neither is better or more important than the other. We find them both in Jesus in equal measure. Both are required for a Christ-like life. And both are essential for us to impact the lives of those around us and transform our culture as Jesus said we are to do.

Our culture, our own experiences, and too often the church can set us up to think about grace and truth as an "either-or" choice when what we see consistently in the life of Jesus is "both grace and truth," not one instead of the other or one more than the other but both together in equal measure. What might happen if the church of Jesus Christ was not afraid to love like Jesus and was not ashamed to speak the truth like Jesus? His grace and truth changed the world once before. And I believe if we get it right, his grace and truth can change the world again through us.

# Reflect

o In what ways do I show grace?

o In what ways do I proclaim truth?

o Do I tend to be more of a "truther" or a "gracer"?

o What can I do to grow as a person who balances grace *and* truth?

# 2.
# Why Grace Is Essential
# and Truth Matters

If we are to have an impact on our world the way Jesus did, then we must possess his compassion for people and his passion for truth. Both are equally important for those of us who want to represent him well and care for people the way he did. Let's consider why each one is critical to our faith.

## Why Grace Is Essential

Grace seems the right place to start as we think about following Jesus faithfully. For two thousand years, when people have heard the name *Jesus*, they have thought about the greatest love the world has ever known. My hope and prayer is that one day soon, even if they disagree with what we believe, when people hear the word *Christian*—they will immediately think of people who love as selflessly and as sacrificially as Jesus did. Why must we be people of grace?

*1. Jesus commanded us to be compassionate and extend grace.*

Jesus taught that the second most important commandment is "'Love your neighbor as yourself'" (Matthew 22:39). Nothing is more important, according to Jesus, except the command to love God with the entirety of our being. He also instructed us to "Do to others as you would have them do to you" (Luke 6:31). Loving others is not optional for Christ's followers. It's essential.

Jesus also told his disciples, "By this everyone will know that you are my disciples, if you love one another" (John 13:35). He didn't say everyone will know you are my disciples if you get your doctrines right or hold fast to the truth or refuse to compromise your principles. All of those are important. But Jesus said the primary trait that will grab the attention of the world is love.

Francis Schaeffer, an insightful Christian philosopher and a champion of traditional Christian beliefs, wrote: "There is nothing more ugly than an orthodoxy without understanding or without compassion."[1] *Orthodoxy* is the term used to describe the historic Christian faith. It's the faith of the Apostles' and Nicene Creeds. It's the theology that the church has held onto for two thousand years and that you find in the writings of great theologians and church leaders such as Saint Augustine, Martin Luther, John Calvin, and John Wesley.

But Schaeffer, who was thoroughly orthodox himself, wanted Christians to understand that as important as it is for our beliefs to be true to what the Scriptures teach, it's not enough. Correct doctrine is critically important but not sufficient for us to live and minister as Jesus did. Holding and contending for the truth without compassion doesn't make us faithful disciples. In fact, if doctrine is all we get right, we are very likely to come across as little more than ugly and hard and mean. Sadly, this is how many people, especially young people, have come to see those of us who call ourselves Christian—and not without reason. All too often those who represent the church—frequently in the media—speak about difficult, emotional topics and seem

Holding and contending
for the truth without compassion
doesn't make us faithful disciples.
In fact, if doctrine is all we get right,
we are very likely to come across
as little more than ugly
and hard and mean.

to be much more concerned about speaking the truth than they are about those to whom they are speaking. Richard Needham of *The Toronto Globe and Mail* wrote: "The man who is brutally honest enjoys the brutality quite as much as the honesty. Possibly more."[2]

Those of us who are passionate about the truth need to be certain that we are never brutal or unkind or unfeeling when we speak truth to others. That's not the kind of "truth-telling" that we see in Jesus. And we should be careful that others never see that kind of "truth-telling" in us.

## 2. Truth without love is a lie.

Another reason we must be people of grace is because the truth spoken without love is a lie. I read this paradoxical statement somewhere many years ago, and I have thought and spoken about it so often that I think I understand it. I believe it means that God intends truth to be a blessing in our lives. Sometimes truth is hard to hear, but God speaks truth into our lives not to tear us down but to build us up; not primarily to make us feel guilty but to move us to confession and repentance so that we can experience forgiveness; not to take life from us but to bring us into the abundant life that is ours in Jesus Christ.

When we speak the truth without love—when we speak truth without real concern for the other person's well-being— then we're using truth for a purpose for which it was never intended. And in so doing, the truth we speak becomes something different than what God meant it to be.

When God gives us truth to speak into another person's life, it's not so we can stand above her and wag a finger in her face. It's so we can stand beside her and put an arm around her shoulder.

Many years ago I heard a story about two pastors. One had left the church he had served for many years and the other had taken his place. A church member was asked if she hated to see the old pastor leave. "I think the change will be good for the church," she said. "Frankly, I was tired of all the hellfire and brimstone." The questioner then asked, "So, the new pastor doesn't talk about hell?" And the church member replied, "Oh, he talks about hell. But when he does, there are tears in his eyes."

Romans 8:1 says, "Therefore, there is now no condemnation for those who are in Christ Jesus." God brings truth into our lives to convict us, not to condemn us. Conviction tells us that we have done wrong but also that we can do better. Conviction tells us that we have sinned but also that we are loved. Conviction makes us face ourselves and then turns us to the face of a gracious God who is more willing to forgive than we are to ask for forgiveness. Conviction is the truth that a God who weeps for us brings into our lives.

Condemnation, on the other hand, is very different. Condemnation comes into our lives to shame us and defeat us and demoralize us. Condemnation rejoices in pointing out our sins and delights in exposing our guilt. It has no redemptive purpose and cares little for the person it attacks.

What we are promised in Romans 8 is that God brings his truth into our lives not to condemn us but to convict us. Any time we speak the truth in a way that is condemning and meant to shame another person, we are not speaking the truth the way that God would. And for that reason, it's not the truth at all.

### 3. Grace often enables people to hear the truth.

A third reason grace is essential is because "Nobody cares how much you know, until they know how much you care."[3] That's an old line attributed to Theodore Roosevelt, and it's true.

Who were the ones most open to Jesus when he walked the earth? Who opened their lives to him and listened to him and fell in love with him more than anyone else? It was that group of people referred to in the Bible as "the sinners."

There was actually a large group of people in Jesus' day referred to as "the sinners." They simply could not do all that the Law required. Uneducated, poor, and often overwhelmed by the burdens of making it day to day, they could never seem to live up to the expectations of society or the demands of the Law. And they knew it. The "good, religious people" of the day, such as the Pharisees, referred to them as "the sinners," and no doubt that's how they thought of themselves.

It is this group that is referenced in Luke 15:1-2: "Now the tax collectors and sinners were all gathering around to hear Jesus. But the Pharisees and the teachers of the law muttered, 'This man welcomes sinners and eats with them.'"

Though the Pharisees and other religious folks often were scandalized by the ministry and the words of Jesus, it was "the sinners" who sought him out. They were the ones who made every effort to get close to him, listen to his teachings, and spend time with him. What makes that so amazing is that Jesus was consistent in his message. The first words he speaks in Mark's Gospel are "The time is fulfilled, and the kingdom of God is at hand; repent and believe in the gospel" (Mark 1:15 ESV). Here Mark is introducing his readers to the ministry of Jesus, stating right up front that Jesus came preaching that we all need to admit our sins, ask for forgiveness, and turn from the wrongs we have committed.

You might think that the people who had the most to feel guilty about and were thought of as "the sinners" by society— and even by themselves—would be the least drawn to Jesus and his message of repentance. But it was just the opposite. They were attracted to him like no one else. Instead of hiding their sins from him, they opened their lives to him. And more than anyone else, they fell in love with him and followed him.

Why? Because Jesus spent time with them and listened to them. When others condemned them, he told them about a Father in heaven who loved them. When others told them they deserved their diseases, he healed their illnesses. When others attacked them, he defended them. And because they knew Jesus cared about them, they cared about what he had to say when he spoke truth into their lives—even the difficult truth that they were sinners and needed to turn from their sins.

When I was in college, I was a member of the InterVarsity Christian Fellowship. We took our faith seriously and wanted to bring others to faith in Christ. Our strategy for evangelism was to set up a table of Christian books outside the campus bookstore and try to sell them to students as they went by. In other words, our plan for reaching other students was to try to convince them to spend money on books they had no interest in reading.

When students did stop at the table and discovered that we were selling Christian literature, they either moved on quickly or told us why we were foolish to believe in fairy tales about a mythical God. Our response was to tell them why our beliefs were intellectually credible and why their materialistic worldview was lacking and untenable. And there would ensue a philosophical discussion that would quickly turn into little more than our trying to convince our nonbelieving peers that we were better informed and more intelligent than they were.

Guess how many people we saw come to faith that way? You got it. None.

My junior year, we decided that love was the answer. We decided that we needed to focus on loving each other and those who didn't yet believe in Christ. Our emphasis for that year centered on small groups that would study together, pray together, share life together, have fun together, and love one another. And each group was to find some way to share that love with nonbelieving students, such as providing a study break with food and drinks during finals week for everyone in their dorm.

We knew that everyone needs love, and we were convinced that almost everyone will respond to love. We believed that if people experienced real love—the love of Christ—they would be more likely to drop their defenses and listen to what we had to say. Our hope was that they would discover what we had discovered—that what our hearts long for most can be experienced and satisfied through a personal relationship with God through Christ. Someone has said that genuine love is the ultimate apologetic. It's so real and so rare that when you encounter it, it's hard to argue with.

It was a great year, learning to love others in the body of Christ and those who didn't yet know Christ in ways that were caring and practical. At our first meeting the following year, we gathered for worship and Bible study. There were over a hundred of us present. I was leading the meeting, and the worship time was especially powerful. The presence of the Holy Spirit was strong, and the love in the room was palpable. At the end, I said, "Last year we decided that we were going to learn to love each. We decided that if we did that and if we invited non-believers to experience real love with us, they would be more likely to open their hearts to Jesus and his Spirit. I feel that love here tonight, and I feel God's Spirit here tonight. And now we have to invite nonbelievers to join us in these meetings so they can experience what we're feeling right now."

Just then, as if I had planned it, a freshman I had never seen before named Roger spoke up in front of the hundred-plus students there that he didn't know. "Well," he said, "I'm a non-Christian, and I gotta tell you, there's a very cool vibe in here." What he was describing in very 70s terminology was what it's like to be in the presence of love—God's love and the love of God's people.

Roger continued to meet with us, and later that year he trusted in Jesus as his Savior. We continued to emphasize small groups, the importance of sharing life and loving each other, and the necessity of reaching out to those who don't know Christ through practical acts of grace and compassion. Before the year was over, another dozen students also made a commitment to Christ as their Lord and Savior. Trust me, as soon as they did, we got them involved in Bible study and we gave them some of the same books we had tried to sell previously. If you're going to be a committed Christian on a college campus, you had better know what you believe and why you believe it. Truth matters. But those of us who are naturally "truthers" need to understand that most people are not argued, outsmarted, lectured, or guilted into the Kingdom. Most people are loved into the Kingdom.

People do have questions, and honest questions need to be honored and answered. But people are unlikely to care about the answers we provide unless they know that we genuinely care about them and the questions they are asking.

*4. Jesus was motivated by compassion.*

A final reason that grace matters is that it mattered to Jesus. Jesus is our model of the spiritual life, and the grace he demonstrated was motivated by compassion. Spiritual growth is the process of becoming more like Jesus, becoming more conformed to his image inside and out. We are growing spiritually as we learn to see the world the way he saw the world, love what he loved, turn away from the things he turned away from, relate to people the way he did, and become motivated by the same commitments that motivated him. What we see over and over in the Gospels is that Jesus was motivated by compassion. Here are a few examples.

*When Jesus landed and saw a large crowd, he had compassion on them and healed their sick.*

Matthew 14:14

*Jesus called his disciples to him and said, "I have compassion for these people; they have already been with me three days and have nothing to eat. I do not want to send them away hungry, or they may collapse on the way."*

Matthew 15:32

*Jesus stopped and called them [the two blind men]. "What do you want me to do for you?" he asked. "Lord," they answered, "we want our sight." Jesus had compassion on them and touched their eyes. Immediately they received their sight and followed him.*

Matthew 20:32-34

*A man with leprosy came to him and begged him on his knees, "If you are willing, you can make me clean." Jesus was [filled with compassion*]. He reached out his hand and touched the man. "I am willing," he said. "Be clean!" Immediately the leprosy left him and he was cleansed.*

Mark 1:40-42

Throughout his ministry Jesus was motivated by compassion. In the Greek, the phrase that is translated "had compassion" or "was filled with compassion" literally means "to be moved in the inward parts."[4] That's why in some versions you'll find the phrase translated "moved with compassion."

Jesus felt the needs of others deep within himself. He never looked at human need without being moved. He never saw

---

* This phrase appears in a footnote; the text reads "Jesus was indignant."

human suffering without feeling it himself. It was this deep compassion and love, along with his desire to glorify the Father, that caused him to minister grace, healing, and life to others.

The goal of the spiritual life is to become like Jesus, and compassion was central to all that he did. That means there's no living the Christian life unless we feel deeply for others and, being moved by love, care for them and their needs.

Compassion is essential if we are to be faithful followers of Jesus Christ, who offered grace to others. But truth is no less important. After all, Jesus told us that it is "the truth" that sets us free (John 8:32). People are not likely to listen to the truth unless we share it with compassion. But grace alone, as essential as it is, is not enough. People also need the truth.

We see in Mark's Gospel how beautifully Jesus combined grace and truth when he saw a crowd that had come to hear him teach:

> *When Jesus landed and saw a large crowd, he had compassion on them, because they were like sheep without a shepherd. So he began teaching them many things.*
>
> Mark 6:34

Jesus looked upon a large crowd of people who were without a shepherd. No one had taught them who God is. No one had told them how to discern truth from error. No one had taught them how to walk in paths of righteousness or how to find to find green pastures and still waters where their souls could be nourished. No shepherd had told them what they needed to know to walk through the valley of the shadow of death without fear. The same compassion that caused Jesus to heal the sick and feed the hungry, the same compassion that moved Jesus to raise a dead boy and give him back to his mother, the same compassion that led Jesus to embrace a leper and make him whole caused Jesus to begin "teaching them many things." Jesus' heart of grace moved him to speak spiritual and moral truth into the lives of people who needed to hear it.

Grace and truth are not in competition. They are partners in creating a beautiful life that looks like the life of Jesus and ministers the way he did.

## Truth Matters

We've considered some reasons grace is essential. Now let's look at why truth is equally important. Throughout the ages, ordinary people, great thinkers, and philosophers have struggled to answer the same question Pilate asked Jesus: "What is truth?" There are many opinions and beliefs regarding the nature of truth and how it is determined. As a Christian, I believe that all truth comes from God (who exists outside of us and is independent of our experiences) and from his revelation of himself. This revelation has been made known to us through his written word and through the Living Word, Jesus Christ. Spiritual beliefs and moral values that accurately represent God's nature, thoughts, will, and actions as revealed in the Scriptures and the life and teachings of Jesus are true. I acknowledge that there are differing views on the authority and interpretation of the Scriptures among Christians; but as a classical Christian who holds to the traditional beliefs of the Christian faith, I believe that the Bible is the highest authority for understanding truth and determining our Christian beliefs. As a follower of Jesus in the Wesleyan tradition, I also affirm the importance and value of allowing tradition, reason, and experience to inform our understanding of the Scriptures. To put it in the simplest of terms, however, God has told us how we are to live if we are to please him. When we conduct ourselves in keeping with what God has revealed to be acceptable to him, we are walking in truth.

## 1. *Spiritual and emotional growth require truth.*

One reason truth is so important is that all significant spiritual and emotional growth require truth. After more than thirty years of being a pastor and being invited into the secret lives of people, I am convinced there is no deep, authentic spiritual growth in persons' lives until they are willing to be honest with God and with themselves. I don't care how much you pray, read the Bible, serve, or attend worship; if you are not willing to look at the truth about yourself and be honest about that truth, you will never experience real, transforming spiritual or emotional growth.

Sometimes I wish that I had never read the New Testament and that people in the church I serve had never read it either. I know that's a strange thing to say. What I mean is that I wish we could read the Gospels as if we had never read them before. Many of us are so familiar with the story that we tend to overlook what Jesus said and did that would surprise us, maybe even disturb us, if we were reading it for the first time.

If you had never read the Gospels and I gave you a New Testament, inviting you to read about the most loving, gracious man who ever lived, I think you'd come to some passages that would shock you or at least cause you to scratch your head and ask, "How does that make any sense? Isn't this guy Jesus supposed to be compassionate and caring?"

For example, in John 8 we read about the woman who was caught in adultery. The Pharisees and teachers of the Law dragged her before Jesus and made her stand before a crowd while accusing her of immorality and threatening to stone her to death. First, Jesus defended her and said, "Whoever hasn't sinned should throw the first stone" (John 8:7 CEB). When the crowd dispersed, he showed her compassion and said, "Neither do I condemn you." And then he continued. "Go, and from now on, don't sin anymore" (8:11 CEB).

Like all of us, this woman needed to be told to turn from her sins, but I wouldn't have done it the way Jesus did. I think I might have spoken truth much more gently and slowly into this woman's life. I mean, there she was, having been shamed before a crowd, the pawn of cynical men. She probably had been used and abused by men most of her life. And just five minutes before, she was terrified that she was about to be stoned to death. If I had been in Jesus' shoes, I think I might have said something like this: "God loves you. You are dear and precious to him. I want you to follow me and learn about a God of mercy who cares about you deeply and can change your life. There are a number of women who are my disciples. They are beautiful women of God. You'll like them. One of them is Mary, and she has had a life much like yours. I'll ask her to look after you. Let these women rub off on you. Listen to what I teach. You'll be amazed how your life can change."

I think I would have said it that way because that's what compassion tells me to do. But that's not what Jesus did. He told her the truth she needed to hear immediately and forcefully: "Stop sinning."

Another example is found in Luke 12. In front of a large crowd, a man called out to Jesus, "Teacher, tell my brother to divide the inheritance with me" (v. 13). Again, if I had been in Jesus' shoes, I probably would have thought to myself, *I better be careful with this one. For a guy to air his family laundry in front of so many people, he's bound to be hurting.*

So I might have put on my empathy hat and said something like, "Friend, I have a brother. Believe me, I know how difficult they can be. I feel for you." Or I might have put on my counselor's hat and told him, "Sounds like you're going through a really rough time. I can feel how much you're hurting. Let's get together in my office tomorrow and see if we can't get you to a better place emotionally." Or I might have put on my mediator's cap and said, "This doesn't have to be win-lose. Bring your brother to see me. I'm sure the three of us can create a solution that's just and fair. This really can be a win-win situation."

I think I would have taken one of those three approaches with this man. But not Jesus. He didn't put on an empathy hat or a counselor's hat or a mediator's hat. He essentially pulled out a boo-yah bat and hit the guy upside the head.

Jesus told him, "Take care! Be on your guard against all kinds of greed; for one's life does not consist in the abundance of possessions" (Luke 12:15 NRSV). In other words, "Look, buddy, there's something more important than what you fill your wallet with, and that's what you fill your heart with. I don't care how much money is in your bank account when you leave this earth; if you die with greed and anger in your heart, you will die a bankrupt man. Deal with your real problem; and your real problem is not your brother. It's you! Boo-yah!"

Really, Jesus? That's what you went with? Where's the love and compassion?

Then there's my favorite example found in John 5. Jesus approached a paralyzed man who had been lying by the pool of Bethesda for thirty-eight years, waiting for his turn to be healed. And Jesus began by asking what might seem to be the most absurd question in the entire Bible: "Do you want to get well?" (v. 6). It seems like a foolish question until you realize that some sick folks don't want to get well. But that's another topic.

The man responded by telling Jesus all the reasons he hadn't been healed. Finally Jesus cut him off and told him to "Get up! Pick up your mat and walk" (v. 8). And he did!

Now here's the strange part. Later that day, Jesus found the guy in the temple, and what do you think Jesus said? Did he say, "God is good all the time," or "How's the first day of the

Why did Jesus speak difficult truths
into the lives of people?
Because people need the truth
in order to grow spiritually
and emotionally.

rest of your life?" or "How are the new legs? Do they feel OK, or do you need an adjustment? I do second touches. Just let me know."

No. Not even close. John tells us: "Later Jesus found him at the temple and said to him, 'See, you are well again. Stop sinning or something worse may happen to you'" (v. 14).

Unbelievable. This poor man had been paralyzed for thirty-eight years. He had been on his feet, healed, for maybe a couple of hours. And the first thing Jesus told him is, "Look, you think you've had it bad all these years? You better get your life right or what you've been through will be a walk in the park compared to what may happen to you."

We read that and we think, *Where's the compassion we've come to expect from Jesus?* Actually, there's no place in the Gospels where you will find Jesus any more compassionate than he is right here. That's because sometimes the most compassionate act you can perform is to tell people the truth they need to hear.

Why did Jesus speak difficult truths into the lives of people? Because people need the truth in order to grow spiritually and emotionally. And why did he at times speak truth so straightforwardly, even harshly? Because people will do all they can to avoid the truth they need. American journalist Herbert Agar put it well: "The truth which makes men free is for the most part the truth which men prefer not to hear."[5]

True spiritual and emotional growth is impossible unless we are willing to be honest about what is most true about ourselves. We can listen to a thousand sermons, read every self-help book that has ever been published, and study the Bible from dawn to dusk; but unless we are willing to look at our failings, immaturity, selfishness, dishonesty, and pride, we will never grow spiritually or emotionally.

The problem is, as T. S. Eliot wrote, that humankind "Cannot bear very much reality."[6] We don't want to see the wrong things we do, much less the wrong things we are. We don't want to be naked before God or others or even ourselves. And so, like Adam and Eve in the garden, we cover up, hide, and pretend. And when we do, we live lives that are false, stop growing spiritually, and fail to become persons of integrity. We all need the truth about ourselves to be made so plain to us that we quit playing games and lying to ourselves.

Russian author Fyodor Dostoyevsky's understanding of human nature was deep and insightful. Much of it he gained through his own struggles, failures, and redemption. In *The Brothers Karamazov* he writes,

> The important thing is to stop lying to yourself. A man who lies to himself, and believes his own lies, becomes unable to recognize truth, either in himself or in anyone else, and he ends up losing respect for himself as well as for others. When he has no respect for anyone, . . . in order to divert himself, . . . he yields to his impulses, indulges in the lowest forms of pleasure, and behaves in the end like an animal, in satisfying his vices. And it all comes from lying— lying to others and to yourself.[7]

The cornerstone of genuine spiritual and emotional growth is honesty. Real, life-giving, spiritually transformative change requires looking honestly at the truth about ourselves. Jesus knew this.

As we saw earlier in the chapter, the very first words Jesus speaks in Mark's Gospel are a call to repent: "The time is fulfilled, and the kingdom of God is at hand; repent and believe in the gospel" (Mark 1:15 ESV). In other words, look at the truth about who you are and where you are. And where you're wrong with God and with others, get right!

Jesus said, "And you shall know the truth, and the truth shall make you free" (John 8:32 NKJV). But often we don't want to hear or admit the truth. Jesus knew that. So he was committed to speaking the truth as plainly and forthrightly as necessary.

Likewise, there will be times when you and I will need to speak the truth that people need to hear—not to be cruel, not to make ourselves feel good or superior, but because love demands that we do so. I can love you for a long time before I tell you the truth you need to hear. But if I never speak the truth you need in order to grow spiritually and emotionally, can I truly say that I love you? Love often requires speaking the truth, and we are always to speak the truth in love.

## 2. Ideas have consequences.

Another reason truth matters is because the thoughts and ideas we entertain and nurture determine how we live. British philosophical writer James Allen wrote: "You are today where your thoughts have brought you; you will be tomorrow where your thoughts take you."[8]

The apostle Paul also wrote about the impact of our thoughts upon our lives. He told the church in Rome, "Therefore, I urge you, brothers and sisters, in view of God's mercy, to offer your bodies as a living sacrifice, holy and pleasing to God—this is your true and proper worship. Do not conform to the pattern of this world, but be transformed by the renewing of your mind" (Romans 12:1-2). In this passage Paul encourages the Roman believers to live in a manner that is worthy of their commitment to Christ. First he states it positively, telling us what we are to do: offer our bodies as living, holy, and pleasing sacrifices to God. Then he states it negatively, telling us what we are not to do: do not conform to the ways of the world. The clear message is that we are to live differently than those who have not put their faith in Christ.

How does this happen? Where do we start? Paul wrote, "Be transformed by the renewing of your mind" (v. 2). Our lives begin to change when our thinking changes. Why? Because ideas and beliefs have consequences.

A well-known saying is often attributed to Ralph Waldo Emerson: "Sow a thought and you reap an action; sow an act and you reap a habit; sow a habit and you reap a character; sow a character and you reap a destiny." Where do our destinies begin? With our thoughts. Ideas and thoughts have consequences. And different ideas and thoughts have different consequences and lead to different destinies. Thoughts that are based on truth will lead to lives that are based on truth. Beliefs that are right (that are in line with the truths Jesus taught and lived) will lead to lives that are right (lives that imitate Jesus). But thoughts and beliefs that are false and wrong will lead to lives that are false and wrong. And there is no time more important to believe what is true than when it comes to thinking about who God is.

A. W. Tozer expressed it well when he wrote, "What comes into our minds when we think about God is the most important thing about us. . . . The most portentous fact about any man is not what he at a given time may say or do, but what he in his deep heart conceives God to be like. We tend by a secret law of the soul to move toward our mental image of God."[9]

For many years, the cover of *Life* magazine each December featured a religious question that people all around the world were asked to answer. One year it was *What is the soul?* Another year it was *Understanding the mystery of Jesus—Why does it matter today?* The most compelling issue was dedicated to answering the question *Who is God?* That year twenty-four very different people gave twenty-four very different answers. I'd like to share some of their ideas about God. Notice how different ideas create very different emotions and behaviors.

Ramon Correa, a twenty-one-year-old thief and murderer living in the slums of Medellín, Colombia, said: "God pardons everyone who seeks him, so pretty much you can do what you want. He is very understanding."

Baldeva Ram could not have had a more different understanding of God. Ram was a middle-aged beggar sitting beside the Ganges River in a wheelbarrow, his fingers and toes eaten away by leprosy. "Brahma," he said, "has written out my fate. I am being punished for sins I must have committed in my last life. God is vengeful. He really punishes."

Sheik Ahmed Ibrahim spent eighteen years in an Israeli prison for terrorism. He stated, "I am ready to kill and be killed myself in fighting the jihad—the holy war—because it is Allah's wish. . . . Killing for the jihad is a holy deed."

Hollywood producer Lynda Sparrow was quoted as saying, "I do believe in a God. But I don't know how to be a Jew, and I don't even know what my soul is. I can't make a connection with God. It's a hopeless feeling that I'm all on my own. . . . I want my daughter to know about God because I don't want her to be in the terrible place I'm in."[10]

Do you see how beliefs determine our lives? Ramon Correa said that he could do anything he wanted because God would forgive him. And so he felt free to harm others and do what he knew to be wrong. Baldeva Ram believed that a vengeful God was punishing him with leprosy because of sins he committed in another lifetime. Do you think his internal life would have been different if he had believed that when God walked the earth in the person of Jesus, he put his arms around lepers and loved them until they were well? Sheik Ibrahim's understanding of God made him willing to kill in the name of his religion. Lynda Sparrow had everything the world says a person needs to be happy, but because she did not have a close connection with or clear understanding of God, she felt hopeless and alone.

Because we are rational creatures, our ideas impact our lives—and none more than what we hold to be true about God.

When believed, false ideas create false and broken lives—some leading to hopelessness and despair; others leading to lives of cruelty and brutality. In the same way—with an opposite effect—true ideas, when believed, can create lives that are true and strong and whole.

Truth matters, and what we believe to be true matters, because our beliefs determine how we live.

### 3. A lie unchallenged often becomes accepted as reality.

A third reason truth is important is that it keeps us from accepting lies as reality. In his first letter to the Corinthians, Paul told the believers in Corinth: "Don't you know that a little yeast leavens the whole batch of dough?" (1 Corinthians 5:6). The idea here is that a little influence over time can have a powerful ability to change something much larger than itself. A lie that is told and not corrected is like a virus on your computer. It corrupts the whole system, and it can spread to others who are connected to you—and then to others who are connected to them. Likewise, falsehoods about who God is, what pleases him, and what it means to live well—unless corrected—act like parasites looking for a host—usually the weak, the unsuspecting, and the innocent. They infect their victims, destroying them from the inside.

John Donne, the seventeenth-century English poet, wrote these familiar words: "No man is an island."[11] Before I read Donne's Meditation XVII in its entirety, I assumed he was simply saying that we all need someone else—that none of us does well alone. That's true, but that's not what Donne had in mind. The lesson he was trying to teach is much more profound and becomes clear when we look at what followed: "No man is an island, entire of itself; every man is a piece of the continent, a part of the main."[12]

Donne wasn't saying that we all need others; that's a given. What he was saying is that we are all connected to each other. We are not islands separated from each other by the sea; we are different parts of the same continent. We are threads in a social fabric, all intertwined and bound together. So what happens to someone else, or what someone else does, affects all of us.

Donne concludes his thought with these words:

> Any man's death diminishes me, because I am involved in mankind, and therefore never send to know for whom the bell tolls; it tolls for thee.[13]

When truth dies in one of us, the bell tolls, telling us that the whole human race has died just a bit. When a lie is accepted as reality, when it is woven into the social fabric, all of society is corrupted just a bit. When morality is changed to fit the moment, then it is cheapened for all of us. And if no one speaks the truth, then the bell tolls for everyone because all of us have been diminished.

There are lies that are prevalent in our culture and even in the church, and if we do not speak the truth against them, they will be accepted as reality. One of the most common lies is the idea that the quality of your life will be determined by the money you make and the possessions you acquire. That's not true. The quality of your life will be determined by the quality of your relationship with Jesus Christ. The quality of your life will be decided by whether you can die to your pride and become a servant to a godly cause that is greater than yourself. The quality of your life will depend upon whether you can let go of the things that others hold dear in order to take hold of things that most people in our materialistic culture do not value. Materialism is a lie, and the people of God need to speak and live against this lie in order to expose it for what it is.

Another lie that is making the rounds again is that there is no hell, no eternal separation from God. I wish I could believe that. I have family members who do not believe in God and are living apart from him. It would give me great comfort to believe there is no hell. But I can't believe that because the One I trust to tell me about heaven, Jesus, spoke more often and in more detail about hell than anyone else in the Bible. And I am convinced that statements that contradict what Jesus taught are wrong and ultimately harmful to people seeking spiritual truth.

Another popular lie is that God doesn't care about sex between two people as long as it's within a loving, caring relationship and doesn't hurt anyone. This lie is built on an incredibly shallow, anthropocentric concept of sin. Sin may hurt people, but that's not ultimately what makes an act sinful. Sin is sin because it is disobedience to God, because it exerts our independence from the God who gave us life and to whom we belong. Romans 3:23 says, "For all have sinned and fall short of the glory of God." The Greek word for *sin* in this verse simply means "missing the mark."[14] Even if an act or attitude does not harm another person, if it misses the mark of God's will for our lives—if it is contrary to what brings glory to God—then it is sinful.

People often wonder, *How can something be wrong if it makes someone happy?* I believe God wants us to be filled with the joy that comes from having an abundant life in Christ. But God is more concerned with making us holy than he is with making us happy. True joy is the by-product of being in a right relationship with God that is transforming our lives. Happiness is not the goal of our lives; holiness is. So whether some action makes us happy is not the way we determine God's will for our lives. We don't look to ourselves to determine God's will; we look to God. That means we look to what he has revealed in Jesus and in the Scriptures, and the Bible states that what we do with our bodies matters. First Corinthians 6:19-20 tells us, "Do you not know that your bodies are temples of the Holy Spirit, who is in you, whom you have received from God? You are not your own; you were bought at a price. Therefore honor God with your bodies." What we do with our bodies matters. Our first question should always be, "Does this glorify God?" not "Will this make me or someone else happy?"

Another falsehood repeated often today is the statement "All gay people are born gay." This statement has been repeated so often that if you say it's not true, you are considered unenlightened, mean-spirited, or hateful. Actually, many scientists believe that nature and nurture both play complex roles in determining sexual orientation. Even the American Psychological Association does not claim to know what causes a gay, lesbian, or bisexual orientation. Here's what the APA does state:

> There is no consensus among scientists about the exact reasons that an individual develops a heterosexual, bisexual, gay, or lesbian orientation. Although much research has examined the possible genetic, hormonal, developmental, social, and cultural influences on sexual orientation, no findings have emerged that permit scientists to conclude that sexual orientation is determined by any particular factor or factors.[15]

Persons who possess a traditional Christian understanding that sexual relations outside of marriage are displeasing to God must be very careful not to stereotype gay persons or say anything that would add to the emotional, verbal, or physical abuse that gay persons have too often suffered.

And we must be careful never to portray homosexual sin as worse than heterosexual sin because that is not what the Bible teaches.

But those on the other side also need to be careful. It's simply not true that science tells us or that "everyone knows" that all gay persons are born gay. Maybe one day science will discover that we are born with an inherent sexual orientation. But until then, it is a falsehood, and a dangerous one, to tell gay persons who want God's will for their lives that science tells us that they were created gay by God.

There is an apocryphal story about a righteous man who traveled to an ancient Jewish city. He was grieved when he saw how wicked the people there were. He walked through the streets of the town, crying out, "Men and women of this wicked city, turn from your evil ways. What you are doing is an offense to God."

First, the people ignored him. When he persisted, they took notice and laughed at him. But he continued to shout, "Turn from your evil ways. What you are doing will bring God's judgment." The people became angry with him and told him to stop. Finally, they began to mistreat him and even beat him. But he continued to preach his message.

One day a child stopped him. "Old man," he said, "don't you see it's useless? No one is listening. Why do you continue to shout?"

The man replied, "In the beginning, I cried out, thinking that I would change them. Now I cry out so they will not change me."

Why must we continue to believe and speak the truth whether or not people listen? So we will remember that a lie is still a lie no matter how many people believe it. And so that our children will know that wrong is wrong no matter how many people say it's right.

Calling a lie true doesn't make it true no matter how many people believe it or repeat it. But a lie told often enough can become accepted as reality. In fact, a lie doesn't have to be told very often to be accepted as the truth if no one challenges it. We must speak the truth not only to change our culture but also so that the lie doesn't change us.

*4. Truth is an essential weapon in our arsenal against evil.*

Finally, truth matters because it is necessary to defeat evil in the world. President Reagan is often given credit for the collapse of the Soviet Union. In his book *Time for Truth*, Os Guinness states that the dynamic that brought down the Iron Curtain and caused the "Evil Empire" to implode had begun decades before the Reagan presidency when men such as novelist Alexander Solzhenitsyn began to speak and write the truth about the evils of the Soviet system, including censorship, torture, and the Gulags.

Writing of Solzhenitsyn and others like him, Guinness observes:

> [They saw] . . . there were only two ways to bring down the mighty Soviet tyranny. One was to trump Soviet force physically, which was impossible for a tiny handful of dissidents. . . . The other was to counter physical force with moral, staking their stand on the conviction that truth would outweigh lies and the whole machinery of propaganda, deception, and terror. They chose the latter, and the unthinkable happened. They won.[16]

After receiving the Nobel Prize in Literature in 1970, the Russian prophet wrote, "One word of truth shall outweigh the whole world."[17]

There is power in the truth, and there is power in telling the truth. It matters that we speak the truth, because that is one of the primary means given to us to fight the lies that mislead, corrupt, and imprison people in darkness. We fight and overcome the wrong within the individual human soul and the corruption within societies and governments by the power of the truth.

I do not expect evil men and women to give way to absolute truth. The power of the truth is not that a Hitler or a Stalin or an Osama bin Laden will necessarily bow to its claims. Its power is that it enables the rest of us to recognize evil when we see it. Its power is that it convicts us that we cannot be neutral toward evil. Its power is that it compels good people to make the sacrifices necessary to defeat evil.

Men and women will not sacrifice all that is dear for beliefs that are nothing more than personal moral preferences. But for the absolute moral virtues of justice and liberty and truth—not only for themselves but also for others—men and women will sacrifice and suffer and give their fortunes and even their lives, counting it a privilege to do so.

## A Gospel of Grace and Truth

The apostle Paul, writing to believers in Rome, must have thought deeply about the message that he was proclaiming and how it would appear to those who would receive his letter. They lived in the world's greatest city, the heart of an Empire with power so immense and vast that it ruled most of the known world. In stark contrast, there was the story Paul had committed his life to preaching: an itinerant Jewish teacher with no formal training gathered a following and in less than three years was put to death, nailed to a cross by Roman authority in the most shameful and painful death that the Empire could

There is power in the truth,
and there is power in telling the truth.
It matters that we speak the truth,
because that is one of the primary
means given to us to fight
the lies that mislead, corrupt, and
imprison people in darkness.

devise—a death that branded him powerless to the Romans and cursed by God to the Jews.

As Paul contemplated all of this, he also must have thought about the lives he had seen changed by the grace and truth of the gospel: adulterers made faithful, the greedy made generous, drunkards made sober, the mean-spirited made kind, the self-centered made open-hearted, and sinners made into saints.

Paul must have thought that for all its power, Rome could never do what the gospel could do: change a human heart, transform a wayward life, bring home the lost, and reconcile a sinful soul to a holy God. So he boldly wrote the words we find in Romans 1:16: "For I am not ashamed of the gospel, because it is the power of God that brings salvation to everyone who believes: first to the Jew, then to the Gentile."

Yes, there is power in the truth and grace of the gospel— God's power. Paul was not ashamed of the truth he proclaimed, and neither should we be.

If you proclaim the truth revealed in the Scriptures—even if you do so with grace—the culture is likely to label you unenlightened and mean-spirited. You may be told that you are on the wrong side of history. But the real question is not what a fallen culture thinks of us. Nor is the question what those within the church who deny the full inspiration and authority of the Bible believe about us. The only question that matters is *What does God think of us?* And if we are people who value and live out grace and truth—not one instead of the other or one more than the other but both together in equal measure—then God will deem us faithful, and we will be on the right side of eternity.

# Reflect

o How well do I demonstrate Jesus' compassion for people? His passion for truth?

o How do my ideas about God impact the way I relate to others?

o How can I show others that I genuinely care about them?

o Am I willing to look honestly at the truth about myself?

o Am I reluctant to confront the lies of our culture with truth? If so, why?

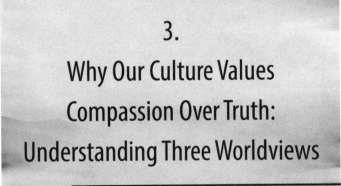

# 3.
# Why Our Culture Values Compassion Over Truth: Understanding Three Worldviews

# 3.
# Why Our Culture Values Compassion Over Truth: Understanding Three Worldviews

Grace and truth—we need them both to be faithful to who God is and to be in ministry to the world in the same way Jesus was. And we need them both for our own lives to function well.

Grace is like a safety net. We all know we are going to fall. We know we will fail ourselves, hurt others, and sin against God. Consequently, we know that there will be many times in our lives when we will need forgiveness, a second chance, and a new start. So, we thank God that there is grace to catch us when we fall.

Truth is different. It's like solid ground that gives us a place to stand. C. S. Lewis wrote that coming to know God's truth "is a delight in having touched firmness; like the pedestrian's delight in feeling the hard road beneath his feet after a false short cut has long entangled him in muddy fields."[1] Truth creates a foundation for our lives that is solid and firm. The great truths about who God is that are revealed in the Scriptures reach all the way down to what is bedrock in the universe. When our lives are founded upon these truths, they are no longer false and shallow and dishonest; instead they become true and deep and authentic.

We all need the firmness of truth beneath our feet. It's how we are made, because we are made in the image of the One who is righteous and true. So we yearn to know what is real and right. See it as a blessing or a curse, but human beings long to know the truth about who we are, why we are here, and what we are meant to accomplish with our lives. We want our lives to matter. This yearning inside us for meaning is an inner voice of wisdom, telling us that it's possible to mark time on this planet for eighty-plus years, collecting accolades and honors along the way, and still live a life that is senseless, shallow, wasted, and small.

If truth is no less essential than grace and we are made with a need to know what is true, then why is there such trouble with the truth? How has our culture come to the place where it not only values compassion over truth but also is disdainful of people who claim to have the truth and is offended by the idea that there are spiritual and moral realities that are true for everyone? The answer lies in the fact that in the latter part of the twentieth century, we in the West exchanged one worldview for another.

A worldview is a lens through which we perceive reality and make sense of the world. It's a set of assumptions, beliefs, and values we use to determine the meaning of our experiences and the validity of competing truth claims. Since the early days of Christianity, there has been a progression from a scriptural worldview to a modern worldview to a postmodern worldview. Understanding each of these worldviews will give us greater insight into why there is such trouble with the truth today.

# A Scriptural Worldview

From the time of its most inauspicious beginnings until the time Christianity became the official religion of the Roman Empire, the Christian faith grew in its cultural influence. For several centuries following the legitimization of Christianity by the Roman government, the Christian faith contributed to the reshaping of the beliefs and values of Western civilization until, eventually, the predominant worldview of the West was a scriptural worldview. The very fact that Christianity became the official religion of the Roman Empire may be the most amazing event in world history. Humanly speaking, there was no reason it should have happened. The Christian faith was begun by an itinerant Jewish rabbi with no political clout. He was found guilty of insurrection and crucified by the Roman authorities. This type of death was a symbol to the Romans of weakness and foolishness, and to the Jews it signified that he had been rejected by God. That's why Paul wrote to the Corinthians, "But we preach Christ crucified: a stumbling block to Jews and foolishness to Gentiles" (1 Corinthians 1:23). The likelihood of a religion that worshiped such a despised character becoming the dominant spiritual force in an empire that worshiped political power and military might was minimal to say the least.

Those who followed Jesus while he was alive were also among the least likely to change the religious ethos of Rome. They were primarily the despised, the uneducated, and the powerless. After his death, most of those who put their faith in Christ through the preaching of his apostles were from the same lower classes of society. Again, Paul wrote to the Corinthians, "Brothers and sisters, think of what you were when you were called. Not many of you were wise by

The Christian worldview had a profound
effect upon Western thought.
Through art and literature and the
teachings of the church, the truths
of the Scriptures influenced and
shaped the way individuals
and culture looked at reality.

human standards; not many were influential; not many were of noble birth" (1 Corinthians 1:26).

For three centuries this small faith was severely persecuted by the Roman authorities, and many of its leaders were martyred. Converts to Christianity were not asked simply to accept the teachings of a deceased rabbi about the importance of kindness, honesty, and loving one's neighbor; they were required to believe the most outlandish claims: Jesus Christ was God in the flesh; he was crucified, dead, and buried; on the third day he physically rose from the dead; his death made atonement for our sins; and by faith in him we can be saved from the penalty for our transgressions. Can you think of a more difficult formula for creating a movement—the promise of persecution and the necessity of believing the unbelievable?

From a human perspective, there was nothing about the Christian faith, its early history, or its converts that would have caused anyone to predict that one day it would become the official religion of the Roman Empire—or that its beliefs would become the formative intellectual framework for an entire culture. But that's exactly what happened. Its influence grew and began to change the Western world until in A.D. 380 the Emperor Theodosius the Great enacted a law that established Christianity as the Roman Empire's official religion.

During this time the Christian worldview had a profound effect upon Western thought. Through art and literature and the teachings of the church, the truths of the Scriptures influenced and shaped the way individuals and culture looked at reality. It would be naïve to think that everyone possessed a Christian worldview, or even that those who did always understood the ethical implications of their faith or lived out the ones they did understand. (We have said that individuals are imperfect works in progress; cultures, if anything, are even more so.) But there came to be a general consensus within Western culture that there are spiritual and moral truths that apply to everyone—moral truths such as the Ten Commandments and the Sermon on the Mount; spiritual truths such as "people are destined to die once, and after that to face judgment" (Hebrews 9:27), "all have sinned and fall short of the glory of God" (Romans 3:23), and "God so loved the world that He gave His only begotten Son, that whoever believes in Him should not perish but have everlasting life" (John 3:16 NKJV).

There was the assumption that these truths could be known because God had revealed them in the Scriptures and in the person of Jesus Christ. It also was generally accepted that these truths about God and what he has done in Christ are the most important truths anyone could know because this world will one day end, but our spirits will live forever.

For a time, the West generally saw reality through a scriptural worldview. Biblical truth was the lens through which people viewed the cosmos, the events of history, and the meaning of life.

## A Modern Worldview

Over time the cultural consensus began to change. Following the Dark Ages, the Renaissance and the Enlightenment (spanning from the fourteenth through the eighteenth centuries) were a time when people began to question the belief that ultimate truth could be found in the Scriptures. There was a new-found confidence in the power of human reason for determining truth. Though originally stated in pre-Christian times by the ancient Greek philosopher Protagoras, the idea that "man is the measure of all things" came to dominate the worldview of influential authors, artists, and philosophers during this period.[2] Inherent in the belief that "man is the measure of all things" is the idea that we can determine truth apart from God. We do not need divine revelation because human beings have the intellectual capacity to determine what is moral and what is true through the power of reason and logic. The way that leading thinkers viewed spiritual and moral truth from the time of the Enlightenment until the mid-part of the twentieth century is referred to as *modernism*. Let me clarify that despite its name, modernism is not the "most modern" or current Western worldview. That would be postmodernism, which is the third and final worldview we will explore. So, what is modernism?

To understand a modern worldview, think Joe Friday of the TV show *Dragnet*. His catch line is remembered as "Just the facts." Actually, what he said was, "All we want are the facts." So, to get a handle on modernism, think "just the facts." Late in the Renaissance and throughout the Enlightenment, the questions that philosophers wrestled with were "What can we know?" and "How can we know that we know it?" In other words, what are the facts of which we can be absolutely certain?

Over time the old answers were discarded and with them a scriptural worldview. The Enlightenment scoffed at the idea that God is the source of truth; that he has revealed these truths to us through his faithful servants, most perfectly in his Son, Jesus; and that we are to use our faith and our intellect to receive God's revelation. Instead of looking to God for ultimate truth, the leading philosophers of the Enlightenment looked to themselves. That's what we prideful, self-centered human beings tend to do. In our personal lives and in our moral philosophies, we decide that "man is the measure of all things," and we give in to the tempter's first promise that if we eat from the tree of knowledge we can determine for ourselves what is moral and what is not and, as a result, become like God—autonomous and free.

In particular, modernism came to hold that something was true if and only if it could be proved by human logic, reason, or science. Very left-brain. Very Joe Friday.

For all of its failings, modernism does claim there are some moral truths that apply to everyone—truths such as we live in the same world and possess the same human nature. Therefore, there are some moral obligations that all of us should live by. Using the power of human reasoning, the leading thinkers of the Enlightenment (also referred to as "the Age of Reason") were certain that we could discover what these ethical truths are.

We certainly can be grateful for the scientific progress that modernism has made possible. Its insistence that there are physical laws and properties that can be understood and manipulated by the human intellect has made possible the incredible technological, engineering, and medical advancements that benefit us all. But there was a huge downside to modernism. It created a worldview that made spiritual matters less certain and, therefore, seemingly less real and less important than physical realities. Since spiritual truths cannot be tested by a scientist, proved by reason, or examined by the senses, modernists believe that questions regarding spiritual reality are not the matters that serious-minded, practical persons need to give much thought. No matter how you slice it, the spiritual world is just so much pie in the sky. Nothing can be known about it, so rational people should put their questions about spiritual reality high on a shelf and leave them there.

In essence, modernism shrunk the cosmos we live in. It removed God from the reality of daily life and, instead of forging a path to brave new worlds, it placed human beings in a universe too small for the human soul to thrive in. We were removed from a cosmos charged with the glory and the purposes of God and dumped into a cold, empty universe.

Modernism came to hold that something was true if and only if it could be proved by human logic, reason, or science.

The latest modernists are represented by those referred to as "the new atheists," their leading apostle being Richard Dawkins. A world-class scientist and Oxford professor, Dr. Dawkins is also an outspoken critic of religion. His best known book is *The God Delusion,* in which he indicates his contempt for religious belief. He writes that he is inclined to agree with Robert M. Pirsig, who said, "When one person suffers from a delusion, it is called insanity. When many people suffer from a delusion it is called Religion."[3] In his typical bellicose style, Dawkins made this statement in an article on science and religion: "It is fashionable to wax apocalyptic about the threat to humanity posed by the AIDS virus, 'mad cow' disease, and many others, but I think a case can be made that *faith* is one of the world's great evils, comparable to the smallpox virus but harder to eradicate."[4]

Modernism can lead to either agnosticism or atheism. With agnosticism, the belief is that we cannot know anything about God. So, we should file away those perhaps interesting but pointless questions about spiritual realities. We can never know the answers and, besides, they have nothing to do with real life. Atheism, the other option—especially as it is championed by the likes of Dawkins—claims that belief in a deity that cannot be seen or scientifically proved is a delusion at best and perhaps better described as mental illness—and in reality a great evil to be eradicated.

Where does that leave us human beings who look for meaning and want our lives to matter? To Professor Dawkins' credit, at least he is honest about where his modern worldview leads. In an online article several years ago, he told an interviewer that the big "why" questions about our existence and purpose are as illegitimate as a question about unicorns. He said, "It's not a proper question to put. It doesn't deserve an answer."[5] A need for meaning and purpose isn't a valid need, according to Dawkins. He says that even asking the question shows a lack of intelligence and is unworthy of serious consideration.

In my ministry I work extensively with men, and I can tell you that the all-too-common pattern we see in men termed a midlife crisis is usually a crisis of meaning. They have done all that is required of other species. They have survived, met their own physical needs, propagated the species, and provided for their offspring. But then they get hit with something no other life form ever encounters: questions about the meaning of life. What's it all for? What does it mean? Has my life mattered? These are questions most people—men and women—face at one time or another.

People never seem so lost as when they have no purpose to live for, and they never seem so alive as when they do. Do you think that's a clue about the reality of our being created for a purpose? Sir John Templeton gets at it this way: "Would it not be strange if a universe without purpose accidentally created humans who are so obsessed with purpose?"[6]

Where does this need for meaning come from? Is it a cruel trick played on us by a universe that Dawkins states has "no design, no purpose, no evil and no good, nothing but blind, pitiless indifference?"[7] Has a universe that has no meaning or purpose created beings that require these very things? Is this an awful cosmic hoax? Or maybe the desire within us for meaning and purpose tells us something very important.

C. S. Lewis wrote, "Creatures are not born with desires unless satisfaction for those desires exists. A baby feels hunger: well, there is such a thing as food. A duckling wants to swim: well, there is such a thing as water. Men feel sexual desire: well, there is such a thing as sex. If I find in myself a desire which no experience in this world can satisfy, the most probable explanation is that I was made for another world."[8]

The modernist worldview, expounded so well by Dr. Dawkins, is not big enough to make sense of you or me. It's not grand enough to explain the desire for meaning and significance that creates the human experience. And it's not big enough for the questions we ask. Thomas V. Morris explained the shallowness of modernism when he wrote, "If a worldview cannot make sense of us, we cannot embrace it as giving us the sense of all else."[9]

The world that modernism has offered us—the world of Joe Friday and Richard Dawkins; the world of facts, formulas, logical principles, and colliding atoms—isn't enough to satisfy the longings of the human heart. The worldview of Dawkins and his ilk is big enough to explain mollusks and fruit flies and frogs, but it's not big enough to explain the needs of human beings for love or truth or beauty. It can't explain why human beings desire to understand the meaning of their lives or why we find it so necessary to be understood by others. It can't explain why human beings must create, or the purpose of art, or why music can make us yearn for something beyond ourselves.

What distinguishes us most from other species is not opposable thumbs or a bigger brain or standing upright but our search for significance—something an atheistic, materialist worldview cannot explain. Modernism cannot make sense of what makes us human.

Despite this major shortcoming of modernism, the emergence of this worldview impacted not only the culture but also the church and its message. In an age that trusted in reason above all else, traditional Christianity seemed anachronistic and out of date. Professing belief in the reality of miracles, in a Creator who is involved with humankind to the point that he would inspire a book about himself, in a God who cares enough about us to become incarnate in the person of Jesus and in the resurrection of the dead—no rational person could affirm such nonscientific tripe.

It was through the influence of modernism that Protestant Liberalism was born. The discovery that the earth was not the center of our solar system, much less the center of the universe, seemed to some people to discredit what the Bible taught and the importance of our planet to whatever deity might exist. The influence of Darwinism and the scientific claims that human beings were the product of blind chance undercut the doctrine that we are made in the image of God. And the supposed insights of Freud that we are controlled by passions and desires about which we have little awareness and over which we have little control caused many to doubt that human beings are truly free to make moral choices. Each of these intellectual events rocked the worldview of thinking, religious persons. Together they seemed devastating to traditional Christian beliefs.

Over time, many Protestant theologians came to redefine "the true message" of Christianity. They still saw great ethical weight in the teachings of the prophets, marvelous beauty in the moral teachings of Jesus, and so much promise in the example that the diverse people of the early church could live together united by the same ideals. They believed that "modern" men and women could value these truths *if* Christianity were freed of other nonscientific, unreasonable beliefs—beliefs such as God fully inspiring a book that reveals his will, the reality of the Incarnation, the necessity of an atonement for our sins, and the claim that miracles (which break the laws of nature), including the resurrection of Jesus from the dead, had actually occurred. What was left? Three great truths: the Fatherhood of God, the brotherhood of man, and the sacred worth of the soul—all fine beliefs, but hardly the robust, powerful faith that the apostles proclaimed with their final breath as they were being martyred.

Protestant Liberalism became accepted by many in the mainline churches as "the new orthodoxy" in the late nineteenth and early twentieth centuries. It was taught in the majority of Protestant seminaries and then propagated in our churches by pastors who had been trained accordingly. And so the prophetic words of the apostle Paul were fulfilled, that in latter times there would be many "having a form of godliness, but denying its power" (2 Timothy 3:5).

As we have seen, both the church and the culture were dramatically impacted by modernism. Those outside the church, in particular, found themselves struggling with a difficult challenge. Where do you go to answer questions about meaning and purpose when the worldview bequeathed to you by your culture rejects spiritual realities? Western culture had discarded a scriptural worldview in favor of modernism. Not wanting to go back to a God who is over us and who holds us accountable for our actions yet not content with a universe devoid of meaning and purpose, where do you look? To postmodernism.

## A Postmodern Worldview

The predominant cultural worldview from roughly the 1960s until now is referred to as postmodernism. Generation X and the Millennials are thoroughly postmodern in how they see the world. To understand postmodernism, don't think Joe Friday. Think Oprah Winfrey. Oprah always wants to know *How do you feel about that?* and *How's that working for you?* Oprah had nothing to do with the formation of postmodernism, but she may be seen as an effective evangelist for its message of relativism—the idea that theological and moral beliefs are valid if they are meaningful to the person who holds them.

Modernism told us that we can't know anything about spiritual matters. Postmodernism reacted by saying, in essence,

"If we can't know anything for certain about spiritual reality, then all spiritual and moral answers can be valid." To their credit, postmoderns believe there is something more to being human than modernism allows. Maybe their hearts don't tell them that we are "fearfully and wonderfully made" (Psalm 139:14), but most sense that we are more than physical bodies living in a material universe and want to live lives of meaning. The problem is that in spite of what they feel in their hearts, their minds—influenced by the remnants of modernism—tell them that we can know nothing for sure about the spiritual universe. The postmodern solution to this dilemma is to believe that if no answer can be known for sure, then we are free to choose any truth we desire; in other words, all answers are equally valid. If you feel good about your truth, then it's true for you. If you think it's working for you, then it is right for you—and no one can tell you it's not.

Though delineating the basic tenets of modernism is relatively easy, describing the primary beliefs of postmodernism is quite difficult because it is undergirded by a general skepticism—not just about religious matters but about what can be known for certain in all fields, including whether human beings even share the same reality. Meaning is found within: events and objects around us have no intrinsic meaning; they have only the meaning we choose to give them. So if two persons give the same object or event different meanings, both are equally right and neither is wrong.

To put it another way, postmodernism rejects the idea that the "truth is out there" and teaches that the truth is "in here." Truth is not objective; it's subjective. It's not determined by a God who is above us; it's determined by the feelings and beliefs within us. So in a postmodern worldview, spiritual beliefs are valid not because they are in line with the character of God or in keeping with what he has revealed, because the truth is not outside of us. A belief is true because it works for us, and this means it brings comfort to our inner world of feelings, generates an understanding that we find satisfying, or creates a path we find personally fulfilling.

Postmodernism also denies that truth is singular. There is no one truth that is true for everyone. Each of us is free to create our own truth. These "different" truths, even if contradictory, are not thought to be mutually exclusive because what is true for you is true for you and what is true for me is true for me. We can have different truths because we are different people with different experiences—so, of course, we will create different truths for ourselves. No truth is better than any other because truth is not conforming our minds to some reality "out there"; it's what feels right "in here." The only truth you may not believe is that you have found "the" truth.

For example, a true postmodern can affirm your claim that Jesus Christ is "the way and the truth and the life" as long as you are claiming that Jesus is your way and your truth and your life. Postmoderns can be happy that you have found a spiritual path in Jesus that works for you. At the same time, they would disagree and might even be offended if you were to claim that Jesus is the way and the truth and the life for everyone and that other spiritual paths (Islam, Hinduism, Buddhism, yoga, Transcendental Meditation, and so on) are incomplete, inferior, or invalid religious options. Why? Because all you can know is what "works" for you; you can't possibly know what "works" for others. According to postmodernism, a form of spirituality is valid if it brings us comfort and meaning, not if it gives us valid information about what God is really like. Truth for postmoderns is much more about feelings than facts.

Khalil Gibran, who wrote *The Prophet*, lived before the postmodern era; but one of his most famous lines exemplifies the relativism of our time: "Say not, 'I have found the truth,' but rather, 'I have found a truth.'"[10] It sounds like the height of humility. But if "the truth" is out there—if there is a reality that is greater than ourselves; if, in fact, this greater reality brought us into being; if this greater reality is a personal being and is moral in character; if he has created us in his image to know him and to be like him; and if he has gone to great, even sacrificial, lengths to make himself and what pleases him known to us—then is it humble to state that his revelation is not *the* truth but *a* truth? When the One bringing that revelation did not claim to be a way or a truth or a life but the way and the truth and the life, doesn't integrity demand that we examine those claims and either reject them as false if they are a lie or embrace them as the truth for all if he is who he says he is?

If you hold a scriptural or even a modern worldview, you may find it difficult to believe that people are sincerely postmodern in the way they look at reality. Let me share with you a couple of conversations I had with two postmodern young adults. I hope you will see that a postmodern worldview is not the epitome of humility or even a generous appreciation for the viewpoints of others. In fact, where it leads is disturbing and dangerous.

On two separate occasions months apart, I had lengthy discussions about morality with two "twenty-somethings." One was an atheist; the other was a Christian asking my advice about entering the ministry. In the course of each conversation I became aware of the moral relativism that undergirded each person's postmodern worldview. To make certain I understood them properly, I asked, "So, according to your worldview there are no overarching spiritual or moral truths that apply to all of us. Each person is free to create his or her own moral universe and every view is as valid and as true any other. Is that correct?" Both answered affirmatively.

Thinking I would now with one question show them the error of their ways and the foolishness of a relativistic approach to moral truth, I asked each one the same question. "So, according to your worldview, why was it immoral for Hitler to exterminate six million Jews? Why was the Holocaust wrong?"

The Christian considering the ordained ministry simply said, "I can't say that Hitler was wrong. I don't know what was in his heart." When I pressed him and asked what could possibly have been in Hitler's heart that would have made the murder of innocent children morally permissible, he responded, "Maybe the reason wouldn't make sense to you or me. But maybe it made sense to him. So, I can't judge that what he did was wrong."

The young atheist responded differently but came down in the same place. "Everyone has the right to believe what they believe and to fight for their beliefs. That's what Hitler did. I would have fought against him, but I can't say that he was wrong. Ultimately, there is no right or wrong."

You may think these two young people are extreme aberrations; but I believe they are canaries in the mine shaft, telling us that there is trouble deep within the moral philosophy of our postmodern culture. They are the natural by-products of a Western culture that doesn't believe in absolute moral or spiritual truth. And their thinking and words tell us where our culture is headed.

We live in a time that when someone claims there are absolute moral and spiritual truths that apply to everyone, he or she is written off as ignorant and uneducated. And if someone should make the claim that what he or she believes is *the* truth, not *a* truth, he or she is immediately deemed guilty of being closed-minded, judgmental, and hateful.

As we've seen, modernism undercut the message of the church by deeming miracles, the Incarnation, and the resurrection of Jesus as intellectually untenable for thinking persons.

The result was Protestant Liberalism—a watered-down Christianity without a God actively involved in human affairs, without the need or the offering of a Savior, and without the power of the Holy Spirit to change hearts and transform lives. Postmodernism is also a threat to the church and its proclamation of the gospel. Those who don't understand postmodernism or appreciate how it has affected the thinking of persons in our culture—even those in the church—may very well be influenced to see spiritual truth as nothing more than individual preferences. And as this happens, more and more Christians will lose their passion for sharing the gospel because our culture has told us that every belief is equally valid, that the only criterion for truth is whether it works for the person who holds it, and that there is no one truth that is big enough to be true for everyone.

We live in strange times. The nuclear blast of modernism has occurred and, though we don't perceive it, its radiation still lingers in the cultural air we breathe. At the same time, we feel the winds of postmodernism raging around us like a moral hurricane, threatening to destroy the theological home we have built for ourselves. Sadly, the church that should protect us is often as radioactive as the culture and as doctrinally flimsy as a cardboard shack.

To withstand the onslaught, we need to understand fully what we're facing. So, now let us compare in detail the current cultural view of truth with a scriptural worldview.

A man was meant to be doubtful about
himself, but undoubting about the truth;
this has been exactly reversed. . . .
We are on the road to producing
a race of men too mentally modest
to believe in the multiplication table.
— G. K. Chesterton[11]

# Reflect

o How have the truths of the Scriptures shaped the way that I look at reality?

o How have I benefited from modernism? What do I see as its pitfalls?

o How have I been influenced by postmodernism?

o What are the challenges and dangers I face as a Christian living in a postmodern world?

# 4.

# Comparing the Cultural Worldview to a Scriptural Worldview

# 4.
# Comparing the Cultural Worldview to a Scriptural Worldview

As we've seen, a worldview is a lens through which we perceive reality and make sense of the world. It's a set of assumptions, beliefs, and values we use to determine the meaning of our experiences and the validity of competing truth claims. All of us possess a worldview.

Some of us are more intentional in creating the lens through which we understand reality than others of us are. The tendency is to see the world in the same way our culture does. That's the easiest way to approach life—adopt the same values and beliefs about reality and what it means to live well as those around us. And that would be the right way to develop a worldview if our culture shared the same values as the kingdom of God. But when you find yourself in a culture that values materialism, hedonism, and individualism; when your culture mistakenly defines freedom as "the ability to do what I want" rather than "the ability to do what I should"; when the common cultural assumption is that the quality of your life is determined by your financial resources rather than your relationship with God and others—then the "easy way" of adopting the cultural worldview as your own is not the "right way" if you desire to be faithful to Jesus Christ and his calling on your life.

That has always been the case. This is why Paul wrote the believers in Rome, "Do not conform to the pattern of this world, but be transformed by the renewing of your mind. Then you will be able to test and approve what God's will is—his good, pleasing and perfect will" (Romans 12:2). Conforming to the pattern (worldview) of the culture does not lead to our thinking God's thoughts or knowing his will. Our minds must be renewed; we must adopt a new way of looking at the world and a new set of values if we are to have any chance of knowing how God wants us to live and then doing his will.

In this chapter I compare the current "cultural worldview" concerning truth, called postmodernism, with a scriptural worldview. The following comparison is not a complete analysis—not even close. But I hope it will provide some handles for you to grasp the significant differences between these two very different ways of looking at the world. My hope is that by the end of the chapter you will better understand why those of us seeking to be traditional biblical Christians so often feel like "aliens and strangers" in the midst of a culture that has come to feel foreign and peculiar.

To help you see where we're going, here are the major distinctions between a scriptural worldview and the cultural worldview:

- A scriptural worldview sees spiritual/moral truth as objective and universal. It believes truth is determined by God and applies to everyone.
- The cultural worldview (postmodernism) sees spiritual/moral truth as subjective and relative. It believes truth is defined by the individual and applies only to the individual and only in the present situation.

Now, let's break down these distinctions and look at them more closely.

## Objective vs. Subjective Truth

*Scriptural worldview: Truth is objective.*
*Cultural worldview: Truth is subjective.*

When the scriptural worldview says that truth is objective, it means that truth is defined outside of and independent from the individual. There is some standard and there is some Standard-giver who is over and above the human individual and the human race.

When the cultural worldview states that truth is subjective, it means that truth is determined within the individual and by the individual. In the cultural view, my experiences, my reason, and my feelings not only help me understand the truth; they actually create what is truth for me.

The scriptural view says that we use our intellect and our experiences to discover truth. The cultural view says that we use our intellect and our experiences to construct what is truth.

Here's the critical difference: the scriptural view holds that spiritual truths and moral values are true because they correspond to reality. There are spiritual and moral truths that exist outside of us. What I believe about them does not determine their validity for me or for anyone else. They exist independent of me and my beliefs about them because they are reality. In fact, these spiritual and moral truths are every bit as real as the laws of nature that make physics and chemistry and geology possible. In a sense, they are even truer because long after this world with its physical realities is gone, the spiritual world with its truths and values will remain.

The cultural view, on the other hand, states that a spiritual truth or a moral value is true because I believe it is true, and it remains true only as long as I believe it is true. There is no real, objective spiritual world out there; there is only the subjective world that I experience. And it is my experience and the meaning I attach to it that determine what is true for me.

Basically, this distinction comes to this: Who determines reality—God or you? Does God determine who we are, or do we determine who God is?

When Moses encountered God in the wilderness, Moses asked God for his name. Moses knew that when he told the Israelites God had sent him to deliver them from bondage, they would want to know which God he was speaking for. Moses wanted to know how to answer them. So he asked God to identify himself by name. "God said to Moses, "I AM WHO I AM. This is what you are to say to the Israelites: 'I AM has sent me to you'" (Exodus 3:14).

In identifying himself to Moses, through Moses to the Israelites, and through Israel to us, God did not say, "I am who you want me to be." He did not say, "I am who your heart tells you I am," or "I will be whoever you want me to be." God is not some celestial co-dependent waiting on us to tell him who he is, what he's supposed to be like, or who we want or need him to be.

"I AM who I AM" (Exodus 3:14). That's who God was. That's who God is. That's who God will be. And it is who God is that determines reality.

You have probably heard people say, "My God is a God of . . ." and they fill in the blank with whatever they have decided a god should be. If that is not the height of arrogance, I can't imagine what is. The idea that a finite, fallen human being would tell an infinite, holy God who he needs to be boggles the mind.

Or perhaps you've heard people say, "The God I worship would never do . . ." What? Something different than what you would do? Something different than a twenty-first-century

God exists over and above us.
And who he is determines what is true.
Everything that contradicts his nature
and character is false regardless of how
true it may seem to you or me.

liberal or progressive would do? We, whether liberal or conservative, don't decide what God should do. He determines what we should do.

God is not made of spiritual Play-Doh™; we don't have the privilege or the power to remold him to fit our fancy. Yahweh is not a Silly Putty™ God we can shape into what we want him to be in one moment and then in the next remake him into our God *du jour*.

Through the ages we human beings have always tried to create our own pictures of God. And when we do, they are remarkably similar to ourselves. It has been said that "in the beginning God created man in his own image, and ever since we've tried to return the favor." In the Old Testament people created deities based on their own ideas and desires. They called them gods, but God called them idols. We are guilty of the same sin when we believe that who God is—and what is morally true—is determined by our reason and experiences. And that is exactly what postmodern thought—and much of progressive theology—leads us to do.

This just in: there is a God, and you're not him. Neither am I. We didn't speak the universe into existence. We don't create truth. We don't decide what is real and what is not. God exists over and above us. And who he is determines what is true. Everything that contradicts his nature and character is false regardless of how true it may seem to you or me.

## Universal vs. Relative Truth

*Scriptural worldview: Truth is universal.*
*Cultural worldview: Truth is relative.*

The scriptural view states there are spiritual and moral truths that apply to all people in all places in all times, while the cultural views says that truth is different from person to person, situation to situation, and culture to culture.

Dr. Allan Bloom spent decades teaching in America's finest universities. In his book *The Closing of the American Mind* he wrote: "One thing a professor can be absolutely certain of: almost every student entering the university believes, or says he believes, that truth is relative."[1]

Have you heard people make statements like these? "I have my beliefs, but who am I to say what others believe is wrong?" "I could never do that myself; it would be wrong for me. But that doesn't mean it's wrong for someone else." When spoken in reference to moral issues, those are the words of someone who believes that truth is relative.

Of course, there is everything right with respecting people who disagree with you. And there is everything wrong with fighting for what you believe without compassion and humility. There is nothing Christian in trying to force others to live how you live. But neither is there anything Christian about denying that there are universal rights and wrongs.

Why does a thoroughly Christian worldview state that there is spiritual and moral truth for all people in all cultures at all times? Because there is one God, and his nature and character determine truth. This is important. God is reality, not my experience of God or my thoughts about God. It is his nature and character that determine what is morally right and spiritually true.

Why is hatred wrong? Because God is love. Why are adultery and betrayal and disloyalty wrong? Because God is faithful. Why are dishonesty and falsehood wrong? Because God is true. Why is bitterness wrong? Because God is forgiving. Why is lust wrong? Because God is pure. That's why our lives work best when we are loving, faithful, true, forgiving, and pure of heart—because that's when we are flowing with reality instead of fighting against it.

Postmodernism believes that
truth is relative and situational.
There are no overarching truths
that provide a moral compass
for all of us. There is no moral north
star by which we all can navigate
our way through life.

Postmodernism believes that truth is relative and situational. There are no overarching truths that provide a moral compass for all of us. There is no moral north star by which we all can navigate our way through life. There are no capital-T Truths that apply to all of us—only little-t truths that we decide are right for us in a particular moment.

So according to a postmodern worldview, you should never say that something is wrong for others just because you have decided it would be wrong for you. Neither should any culture dare to criticize the moral values of another culture. Our histories are different. Our experiences are different. So it is not only expected but also right that our values and morals would be different. It is judgmental and arrogant to think otherwise.

How broad-minded those words sound. How generous of spirit an unwillingness to judge appears. How enlightened and progressive it seems to promote the belief that no person should judge another's actions and no culture can point out the failings of another.

But where does that leave us? Maybe you could never be a racist, but who are you to tell others that racism is wrong? Maybe you would never hunt a species to extinction. Maybe you would never shoot the last bald eagle so it could be stuffed and placed on your mantle. But who are you to say it's wrong for others? Maybe you think women should possess equal rights, but who are you to criticize the Taliban or the mullahs of Iran? Maybe you think it's wrong that some African cultures perform a surgical procedure that removes a girl's clitoris before she reaches puberty—the thought being that if she can't experience sexual pleasure later in life she will be less likely to cheat on her husband and bring shame on her family. That may sound barbaric to you, but it's their culture; and they believe it works for them. Who are the politically correct guardians of abortion on demand in this country to condemn the people in China who often abort a female fetus because they prefer a male child?

Relativism provides no rationale that is able to condemn evil. When there are no moral absolutes over and above us, morality is nothing more than individual preferences and opinions. When there is no longer a "thus saith the Lord," there is only a "thus saith Fred" or "thus saith Judy," "thus saith Western culture" or "thus saith Eastern culture," "thus saith the prejudiced" or "thus saith the progressive," and so on. No one view or source has any higher authority or any more validity than any other. And where there are no universal truths, there is no real right or wrong, only opinions.

Those of us who criticize moral relativism are often portrayed as the morality Gestapo. "You just want to impose your Western values on the rest of the world" is a common charge against those of us who believe there are universal truths. But that's not what we want. As classical or traditional Christians, we desire the values of God's kingdom for the West and for the rest of the world. So many of the values of Western culture are contrary to the Kingdom—our materialism, hedonism, arrogance, and hyper-individualism. We don't wish to export those values to any culture. Christians in the United States can be grateful for the benefits of living in this great country, but we are Christians first. Where our own country or culture is wrong, we must say so. And where other cultures—even those who have had little Christian influence—possess values that are in keeping with God's kingdom, we must commend them. We don't want a Western way of life for others; we want a Kingdom way of life for everyone.

The other objection we encounter when we condemn relativism is this: "You think you know what's right for everyone;

you're trying to push your individual values on others." No, we don't want our values for others. We want the truth for others—and for ourselves. I'm sure I'm wrong in my thinking about many subjects; I just don't know what they are. I know that I am not yet conformed to the image of Christ—not in my thinking or in my actions. So, no, my goal is not for others to think or act just as I do. Where I'm wrong, I hope others will love me enough to point it out to me. And where others are wrong, I hope they will love truth enough to receive instruction and correction. I want to share what I believe is truth with others and I want others to share what they believe is truth with me because, from the bottom of my heart, I believe that truth matters and that each one of us matters.

## Unchanging vs. Ever-changing Truth

*Scriptural worldview: Truth is unchanging.*
*Cultural worldview: Truth is ever-changing.*

To be clear, just because I believe there are absolute truths doesn't mean that I think I have the truth absolutely. I will need to learn and grow my entire life, and so will you. All of us will continually need to correct our wrong ideas about God and about what is truly right and wrong. But what changes is my understanding of truth, not truth itself.

The biblical view of truth was described by Shakespeare when he wrote these words in *Measure for Measure*: "Truth is truth to the end of reckoning."[2] Gary Nicholson expressed the same sentiment about the truths he'd like to forget or change to be more to his liking in his song "The Trouble with the Truth":

Oh, the trouble with the truth
Is it's always the same ol' thing.[3]

If moral truth is founded upon the nature and character of God, then the only way moral truth would change is if God's character were to change. If God is still figuring things out, if he's a cosmic teenager who needs to mature, if his nature is evolving and who he was yesterday is not who he will be tomorrow, then spiritual and moral truth will also change.

Theoretically, that is a possibility. But the Scriptures teach that "he who is the Glory of Israel does not lie or change his mind; for he is not a human being, that he should change his mind" (1 Samuel 15:29). Likewise, God says about himself, "I the LORD do not change" (Malachi 3:6).

If morality is based on God's character and God's character does not change, then what is morally true does not change. In other words, "Truth is truth to the end of reckoning." That means that truth is not determined sociologically; we don't study what people are doing and then decide that if enough people are doing something, it must be right. Truth is not determined democratically; we don't take a vote and the majority determines what's right for everyone else. Truth is not determined by the Supreme Court; we don't wait for its latest pronouncement and then change our views accordingly. Real truth is bigger than that. It's based on the eternal, unchanging character of God. Therefore, what God has revealed to be true remains true. "The grass withers and the flowers fall, / but the word of our God endures forever" (Isaiah 40:8).

Two worldviews are vying for the hearts and minds of those of us who live in the West. Both cannot both be true. One says that moral and spiritual truth is subjective, relative, and ever-changing. The other says that truth is objective, universal, and everlasting. One is based on the experiences and feelings of human beings. The other is based on the character of God. One is sand. The other is rock. Each of us must decide upon which we will build our life.

If morality is based on
God's character and
God's character does not change,
then what is morally true
does not change.

# Reflect

o Have I ever been tempted to remake God into what I want him to be? How?

o How have I encountered relativism? Is there any evidence of relativism in my own thoughts and actions? Am I ever reluctant to say that what I believe is wrong is also wrong for others?

o Do I want a Kingdom way of life for everyone? Why or why not?

o Is my life built upon the character of God or experiences and feelings?

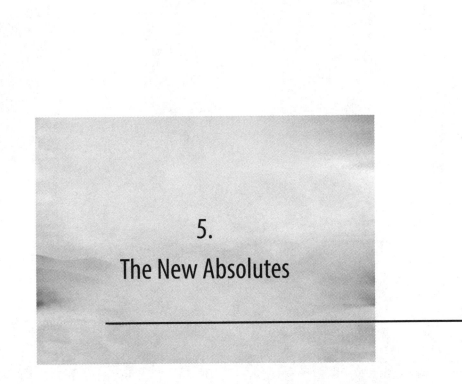

5.
The New Absolutes

# 5.
# The New Absolutes

In light of the fact that the dominant cultural view of truth, postmodernism, holds truth to be subjective, relative, and ever changing, one might think that postmoderns would never claim there are any spiritual or moral truths that everyone must embrace. But actually they do. How does that make any sense? It doesn't. But postmodernism, as it is usually practiced, is inconsistent.

People instinctively know there is right and wrong. For example, most postmoderns would tell you that racism is immoral and evil. But their philosophy gives them no grounds for making that claim. If truth is subjective, then what makes the truth of equality more right than the belief that one race is superior to another? If there are no moral absolutes (such as "all people should be treated equally"), then everyone should be free to determine what is true for him or her and to live that way; and no one should presume to tell others they are wrong.

So what do you do when your conscience tells you one thing ("racism is wrong") and your postmodern thinking tells you something else ("no moral belief is absolutely wrong, including racism")? Most likely you become inconsistent. You argue that some moral choices are so important and obvious that all good people must hold them. These moral values I refer to as the New Absolutes. In our postmodern culture they carry the full weight of universal moral imperatives. And if you think these values aren't viewed as absolutes, just break one. Let's consider them one at a time.

## Openness

The first cultural absolute we will consider is openness, or "being open." Openness is a desired virtue for Christians if defined properly; but, as we will see, postmodernism has redefined what it means to be open.

As it traditionally has been understood, openness means that we hold our views with humility, acknowledging that we have much to learn. In our search for truth, openness is the virtue that moves us to consider ideas about reality no matter the source. After all, God has regularly spoken to his people in unexpected ways and through unlikely sources—even once through a donkey. (As a preacher, there have been some Sundays when I have taken great comfort in that.)

To my knowledge, none of my philosophy professors in college was a Christian. Most of the philosophers we read weren't believers, nor were any of my psychology professors. But my appreciation for truth, for the universe that God created, and for the wonder of what it means to be human was greatly enriched by men and women who did not share my faith.

In the mission work I have done, I have discovered there are incredible lessons to be learned from the poor and the undereducated whose experience of life is so different from mine. You go to help others only to discover that you have received more than you gave and learned more than you could ever teach. So we can believe there is a scriptural worldview that helps us see reality rightly while, at the same time, being open to truth from wherever it may come.

In the current cultural climate, however, openness means something very different. The New Openness insists that we must accept all beliefs—all ideas, theories, or convictions—as equally valid. In *The Closing of the American Mind*, Professor Allan Bloom writes, "Openness used to be the virtue that permitted us to seek the good by using reason. It now means accepting everything and denying reason's power."[1]

The New Openness would have us believe that there are only opinions and feelings that function for us individually as truth—none more right or wrong than any other. In other words, truth is subjective. Furthermore, what was true for you yesterday may not be true for you today, and what's true for you today may not be true for you tomorrow. As your life changes, "your truth" may very well change, so you must stay open.

But as G. K. Chesterton noted, "The object of opening the mind, as of opening the mouth, is to shut it again on something solid."[2] Why are we to be open? So we can find the truth, settle on it, and live by it. As we read in Ephesians 4:14, "Then we will no longer be infants, tossed back and forth by the waves, and blown here and there by every wind of teaching and by the cunning and craftiness of people in their deceitful scheming."

Being open to new ideas is a good trait. But never being able to settle on what is true about God and what pleases him—the apostle Paul doesn't call that "being open"; he calls it being an "infant." And at some point, we all need to grow up. Unfortunately, believing that what God revealed to be true in the past is still true today, and will be forever, is offensive to the sensibilities of postmoderns because it contradicts their understanding of what it means to be open.

Believing that what God revealed
to be true in the past is
still true today, and will be forever,
is offensive to the sensibilities
of postmoderns because it
contradicts their understanding
of what it means to be open.

Professor Bloom critiques the New Openness this way:

> Openness—and the relativism that makes it the only
> plausible stance in the face of various claims to truth
> and various ways of life . . .—is the great insight of
> our times. . . . The study of history. . . teaches that all
> the world was mad in the past; men always thought
> they were right, and that led to wars, persecution,
> slavery, xenophobia, racism and chauvinism. The
> point is not to correct the mistakes and really be
> right; rather it is not to think you are right at all.[3]

The New Openness is built upon relativism, which claims
there are no universal truths. One problem with this view, as he
points out, is that we can never believe with any certainty that
the views we hold are really true. The logical conclusion to this
premise is that there is no reason to try to discover and correct
wrong thinking, whether it's the thinking of others or our own.
If there is no objective standard for truth, how would you ever
know that your new thoughts are more true than the ones you
previously held?

There's another problem with the relativism that underlies
the New Openness: it contains a self-contradiction. Relativism
says there are no universal truths. When you state "there is
no such thing as a universal truth," you are stating a universal truth! It's like saying, "All generalizations are false." It's a
statement that contradicts itself.

"Everything is relative; nothing is absolute," the relativist
says. "A truth is true only for the individual who accepts it as
true. No truth is true for everyone—except for the one truth
that all truth is relative. Why is this one truth absolute and
universal? Well, because I say it is."

Sorry, but you don't get to have your postmodern cake and eat it, too. Either all truth is relative or it's not.

Relativism is self-refuting, and it provides no reason to value the New Openness as an absolute virtue by which to live. Yes, we must be open to all people. And we should always be open to new ideas. But those of us who follow the One who claimed to be the way and the truth and the life simply cannot embrace the mistaken belief that there are no absolute truths that God has revealed about himself. Doing so is not being open. It's being unfaithful.

## Tolerance

Another cultural absolute that is related to openness is tolerance. While openness is centered on ideas and beliefs, tolerance focuses on moral choices (actions) and lifestyles. Like openness, tolerance is a desired virtue for Christians if defined properly. But once again, postmoderns have redefined the term. In fact, the cultural understanding of tolerance has changed so much that practically the worst accusation that can be made about a person in our society today is that he or she is intolerant. Real intolerance is nothing that a follower of Jesus can ever condone because it demeans the worth of someone made in the image of God. And the most detestable form of intolerance or bigotry comes dressed in religious garb.

An example is a remark Jimmy Swaggart made when he was preaching against gay marriage. He said, "I've never seen a man in my life I wanted to marry. . . . If one ever looks at me like that, I'm going to kill him and tell God he died."[4] When your opposition to a practice turns into a mean-spirited attack on the sacred worth of other human beings, it is wrong, hateful, and harmful. And to do it in the midst of a worship service dedicated to a God who loves everyone is blasphemous.

When the religious bigots of Jesus' day wanted to put to death a woman who was guilty of sexual sin, Jesus stopped them and protected her. With persons in his culture who were powerless, marginalized, and even despised—women, children, the poor, persons of different ethnic backgrounds, and sinners—Jesus was incredibly welcoming.

As followers of Jesus we must wholeheartedly embrace true tolerance, which is being willing to "bear" or "endure" (that's the original meaning of the word) a person, an action, or an idea that we do not agree with. In her biography on Voltaire, Evelyn Beatrice Hall, who wrote under the pseudonym S. G. Tallentyre, wrote a statement that describes what we used to think of as tolerance: "I disapprove of what you say, but I will defend to the death your right to say it."[5]

That's how tolerance has traditionally been described—as a willingness to let people be who they are, think what they think, and say what they want to say—even if we disagree. We want that courtesy extended to us, so we should be glad to grant it to others. After all, Jesus commanded us, "do to others as you would have them do to you" (Luke 6:31).

But when postmoderns and progressives promote tolerance, they seem to have something very different in mind. The New Tolerance requires more than allowing someone to say what he wants to say or live how she wants to live. Today's tolerance requires that you embrace and even celebrate the other person's moral choices and lifestyle as being good and right—if for no other reason than the fact that the person believes they are good and right.

In reality, postmoderns—both inside and outside the church—don't actually want true tolerance. In fact, I think it's correct to say that they don't actually believe in it. Real tolerance is thinking that something is less than or different than it should be, and then deciding that you can live with it—

which is far short of embracing or celebrating it. You tolerate only actions or traits you believe to be wrong, bothersome, or undesirable.

Do you tolerate love? Ever heard a wife say, "My husband is so thoughtful, I'll just have to tolerate him"? Of course not. What about integrity or faithfulness? Have you ever heard people say they have a friend with those traits but they'll "tolerate her anyway"? No, because people don't tolerate characteristics and practices that are admirable. You only tolerate persons and behaviors you find lacking or offensive. And that's not what postmoderns and progressives mean when they talk about tolerance. Tolerance for postmoderns is not putting up with what you believe to be wrong. It's believing that something is not wrong at all if someone else believes it to be right. It's the unmitigated affirmation of a person's moral choices even if you disagree with them.

When postmoderns insist on "tolerance," they are demanding something the word has never previously meant. They know that if they can control language and the meaning of words, they stand a much better chance of winning the social argument. So, they have given a new meaning to the word *tolerance*, and they have told us that anything less than their new definition is narrow-minded and mean-spirited.

The obvious example here is the push for gay marriage. It's not enough that society agrees to protect a gay couple's right to live together. It's not enough that society would offer civil unions with the same legal benefits of marriage. The goal of progressives seems to be for homosexual unions to be called marriage. Why? At the risk of oversimplifying the issue (and I acknowledge there are political and legal considerations I am not addressing here), I believe it is largely because they desire the practice of homosexuality to be affirmed as being every bit as valid as heterosexuality.

In the postmodern era there is only one way for traditional Christians to be tolerant on this issue, and that is to deny what we believe to be the clear meaning of Scripture and, without reservation, affirm same-sex relations. You can love persons who are gay and insist on their civil rights, but if you say the practice of homosexuality is displeasing to God, by the culture's definition you are intolerant.

As with the New Openness, there is a philosophical self-contradiction in the New Tolerance. It's a rather interesting dilemma for those who promote it. Should they tolerate intolerance? If all views are equally valid, who can tell the intolerant person that his or her intolerance is wrong? But if the New Tolerance will not tolerate intolerance, then by its own definition the New Tolerance is intolerant. That's what you call a philosophical self-contradiction.

Even in its truest sense, tolerance is not the goal for Christians. Jesus never set the bar that low. Did he command us to "tolerate your neighbor as yourself"? Did he tell us "by this everyone will know that you are my disciples, if you tolerate one another"?

No, he called us to something much higher and much more difficult. He told us to love our enemies, pray for those who persecute us, bless those who curse us. The Scriptures tell us to serve one another, love one another, and even lay down our lives for one another. But tolerate one another? God never made that the goal. As I once heard N. T. Wright say, "'Tolerance' is a cheap, low-grade parody of love."[6]

At the church I serve just north of Houston, Texas, we don't tolerate people. We love people. We love people who believe in Jesus, and we love people who don't. We love people who are white and black and brown and red and yellow. We love people who are straight, and we love people who are gay. We love Republicans, and we love Democrats. We even love people who aren't native Texans. We feel sorry for them, but we love them.

We love people because the God we serve loves people. All people—no matter what they believe or what choices they make. And we desire to be like him.

Tolerate others? God never set the bar that low. He raised it all the way to love. Just put up with someone? That's not the way of Christ; that's the way of someone who can't be bothered. And as his followers, we are called to more.

## Pluralism

Built on wrong concepts of tolerance and openness, another New Absolute is the idea that all religions are of equal validity. It's not hard to understand why this view, called pluralism, has become more popular than ever.

With the increased ease of travel, the multinational nature of doing business in our time, and the vast number of immigrants living within the United States, most Americans now know people who do not share their religious beliefs. And we have found most of these people to be good-hearted, honest, and hard-working. When you know persons of other faiths who share many of your values and who live respectable lives, it can become more difficult to believe that your views are "the truth" and the teachings of other faiths are not.

There's another reason the current culture wants to downplay the differences among the world's religions. We have to find a way to coexist. Sadly, religions all too often have done the opposite. Both in the present and in the past, the belief that one religion is right and others are wrong has led to discrimination, hatred, and violence. I wish I could say that persons calling themselves Christians had never engaged in such evil, but I cannot.

So it is perfectly understandable that people both outside and inside the church want to claim that the world's religions are equally valid paths for approaching God, maybe pointing in slightly different directions, but ultimately leading to the same destination.

Yet the answer to religiously inspired hatred is not to deny our differences or believe a falsehood. If God has truly revealed himself in the life and teachings of Jesus Christ, then the message of the Christian faith is very different from what the world's other religions teach; and the claim that all religions are basically the same and, therefore, equally valid is simply untrue.

Pluralism would require us to believe one or more of the following claims—none of which is intellectually tenable.

*1. All religions teach basically the same thing.*

This statement can be made only by someone who is either ignorant of the world's religions or willing to be disingenuous.

The first question I would ask someone who says that all religions teach the same truths is this: "Do you mean all religions that have ever existed?"

If they said "yes," I would ask them to reconcile the faith of Hindus, who will not kill and eat cattle out of respect for life, with the Aztec religion that the Spaniards encountered when they arrived in what is now Mexico. It is estimated that 20,000 to 250,000 human beings were sacrificed annually by the Aztec royalty because their religion told them such offerings were required by their gods. These sacrifices took place at the same moment in history that Martin Luther was promoting the Protestant Reformation with the central idea that salvation is by God's grace alone, not by human works—and certainly not by the sacrifice of unwilling human victims. You simply cannot say that all religions have taught the same truths.

Others might respond, "Well, maybe not in the past, but presently the world's 'great religions' are basically the same." It is true that Christianity, Islam, Hinduism, Buddhism, and Judaism all teach that we should treat other people as we would like to be treated. But exhortations to be kind to others, work for justice, and care less about the desires of the flesh do not constitute a religion. At best, that's a moral philosophy. Religions claim to do much more than that. They claim to tell us the truth about God.

C. S. Lewis explained it this way: "Christianity claims to give an account of *facts*—to tell you what the real universe is like. . . . If Christianity is untrue, then no honest man will want to believe it, however helpful it might be: if it is true, every honest man will want to believe it, even if it gives him no help at all."[7]

What Lewis wrote about Christianity is true about all the world's great religions. They purport to tell us what is true about the nature of God, the nature of human beings, and how we can enter into a right relationship with the divine. And here the world's great religions could hardly agree less.

Hinduism because of its long and varied history is extremely complex. But, bottom line, its teachings are pantheistic. All that exists is divine. Our human problem is that we don't recognize our divinity.

Buddhism makes few claims about the nature of the divine. Many Buddhists do not believe Buddhism is a religion at all. Its chief concern is not how we can be rightly related to God but why human beings suffer and how that suffering can cease.

Neither of these faiths believes in a personal God who thinks and feels, makes intentional choices, and can be known in a personal relationship. And neither teaches that our problem is

The other great religions base salvation
completely or partially on our good
works and religious deeds.
The Christian faith makes the bold
claim that it is by God's grace alone,
experienced through faith in
Jesus Christ, that we are saved.

that we are sinners guilty before a holy God. Basically the same as Christianity? Not even close.

There are some similarities among the Western religions of Islam, Judaism, and Christianity, which all trace their spiritual ancestry back to a common figure, Abraham. All three claim that there is a personal God and that we have become estranged from him by our sins.

But no other religion teaches that God is a Trinity. No other religion believes that Jesus was God in the flesh or that his death was essential for our salvation. The other great religions base salvation completely or partially on our good works and religious deeds. The Christian faith makes the bold claim that it is by God's grace alone, experienced through faith in Jesus Christ, that we are saved. Not only do the world's great religions not affirm the central tenets of the Christian faith; they are offended by them.

When it comes to what religions actually do—provide us with the facts about what God is like and how we can be rightly related to him—the world's great faiths do not teach basically the same thing. In fact, they could not be more different.

*2. It's a person's sincerity that matters, not what a person believes.*

I refer to this view as "salvation by sincerity." The problem with the belief that "sincerity is what really matters" is that it fails to take seriously that people can be sincerely wrong.

Do you doubt the sincerity of the hijackers who killed three thousand people on 9-11? If someone claims he is killing others for his faith, you may doubt his sincerity. But when someone is willing to kill himself for his faith—that pretty much answers the sincerity question. We can be absolutely certain that the men who flew the planes into the World Trade Towers were sincere in their religious beliefs. And we can be certain that it's possible to be sincere and wrong. In fact, it's possible to be sincere and evil.

Christianity teaches that sincere faith is essential but not sufficient. That's because faith is only as good as its object.

I jumped out of an airplane once. Some guys in my church were going to jump, and they asked me to join them. It wasn't a tandem jump where you're connected to an experienced skydiver. It would be on me, as I was falling to earth for the first time at 120 miles per hour, to pull the cord and save my life. I quickly thought, "If I say yes, I could die. But if I say no, these guys won't respect me." So I did the manly thing and decided I would rather die than be thought of as a wimp. People ask me if I'm going to jump again, and I tell them, "No, my first experience was so exhilarating, I think any future jumps would be anticlimactic." What I'm really thinking is, "I never again want to be that scared little boy in a plane wondering how I ended up doing something this stupid."

Here's the question. What saved me when I jumped? Faith was essential, wasn't it? I had to believe that if I pulled the rip cord, a parachute would open and secure a safe landing for me. I did believe that completely and sincerely.

But what if there had been no parachute in my pack? Or what if the parachute had been too small to slow my fall? Would my sincerity have saved me? No. I would not have died a wimp, but I would have died.

In both jumping out of planes and becoming right with God, sincerity is essential but not sufficient. It matters what you believe in. The object of your faith must be able to save you. If it's not, no amount of sincerity will be effective.

The world's religions offer very different remedies for experiencing salvation. They all insist on sincerity of heart. But the most pressing question is whether the remedy they provide is capable of saving you.

Orthodox Christianity has always made the claim that Christ alone is sufficient for our salvation. Good works, religious practices, and even sincerity of heart will not save us because salvation is not found in us. It's found in Jesus. "Salvation can be found in no one else. Throughout the whole world no other name has been given among humans through which we must be saved" (Acts 4:12 CEB).

*3. No one has the right to judge another person's experiences.*

This belief fits in well with a postmodern approach to reality. It holds that if I experience something as true, then it's true for me; and no one has the right to say it's not.

That's a very naive view of reality. Experiences must always be understood in context. Especially when it comes to matters of religion, our experiences are rarely enough to tell us what's true.

I was once called to the church on a Sunday evening by one of our staff members. She reported that a young man had been led by God to our church. He had been walking for nearly twenty-four hours, and he told her, "The Holy Spirit has brought me here so I can know God." When I arrived, the young man told me what he had told her. Then he stated that the same Holy Spirit that had led him here was now flying above us in the chapel in the form of two birds.

As the conversation progressed, I became convinced he was hallucinating. His religious experience was very real to him. Still, I drove him to the emergency room of a nearby hospital. His mother joined me, and later that night a doctor told us that the man was suffering from schizophrenia and would require medical treatment. Sadly, his mother refused to believe it. Her son said that he was having a religious experience, and she believed his vision was real—just as real, she told me, as

Paul's vision on the Damascus road. She took him home without receiving the medical care he needed.

Was I wrong to "judge" this man's religious experience? It was very real and meaningful to him.

Think of people who have come under the influence of a cult and genuinely believe they are experiencing the words and the presence of God through a leader who later proves to be a fraud. Eventually, they shake their heads and say, "How could I have been so wrong?"

Pastors frequently have conversations with people that begin, "God has told me . . ." After being involved in enough of these conversations, most of us become wary when we hear those words. At times, what is reported does appear to be a real "word from the Lord." But very often what is being reported as a revelation from God is something that isn't consistent with the Bible, and usually it's self-serving.

For example, on several occasions a different man has reported to me that God told him to divorce his wife and marry the woman he was having an affair with. When I began to question these men, each was certain he had experienced God speaking to him. After all, God had already told him the affair was OK because God had said that he wanted the man to be happy. Try as I might, I couldn't convince any of these men that God had not told him to commit adultery and divorce his wife. And try as they might, none of them could convince me that God had indeed told them this. Sometimes it's extremely challenging to help people understand that what they thought was an experience with God actually was something else.

Mature Christians have always understood that our hearts can deceive us, even convince us that God has spoken to us when he hasn't. So we must always ask if our experiences are in line with what God has revealed in Scripture. And we must humbly put our experiences before others and ask for their help in discerning whether what we believe to be God's revelation to us is truly his voice.

There's a famous poem about religious experience usually referred to as "The Blind Men and the Elephant." It's an ancient Indian tale that was translated by John Godfrey Saxe in the nineteenth century. Most often it's used to teach a lesson about religious tolerance, but as I recount it for you, see if you don't discern a deeper meaning.

Six blind men go to see an elephant, each touching it to determine what they can learn about it. The first, feeling its "broad and sturdy side," believes it to be much like a wall. The second feels its tusk and believes it's similar to a spear. The others, touching different parts of the elephant, believe the elephant to be like a snake, a tree, a fan, and a rope. The poem ends this way:

> And so these men of Indostan
> Disputed loud and long,
> Each in his own opinion
> Exceeding stiff and strong,
> Though each was partly in the right,
> And all were in the wrong![8]

The moral of the tale is regularly said to be that all of us have different experiences of God, so we must be humble in our views and not claim that what we believe is any more right than those who have had different experiences. But there is a more profound lesson contained in this poem, and that is how often our individual experiences lead to wrong conclusions about the nature of God.

If you heard someone tell another person that an elephant is like a rope, would you think she had conveyed helpful information? Or if someone told you that an elephant was very similar to a fan or a snake or a spear, and later you saw an elephant for the first time, wouldn't you think, "What was that guy talking about? I would have never found an elephant on my own if that's what I was looking for."

Here's the point. Our experiences are never self-authenticating. In fact, our experiences can provide information that is utterly wrong or so partial in nature that they're not helpful at all. And this is especially true when it comes to spiritual matters that can't be seen with the eye or touched with our hands. In Isaiah we read: "'For my thoughts are not your thoughts, / neither are your ways my ways,' / declares the LORD. / 'As the heavens are higher than the earth, / so are my ways higher than your ways / and my thoughts than your thoughts'" (55:8-9).

In this passage God is saying, "You'll never figure me out on your own—not by your reason or by your experiences. I will have to reveal myself and my ways to you if you are ever going to have a clear picture of who I am and what pleases me."

Humility, real spiritual humility, is more than saying, "I only have part of the truth so I can't say others are wrong." Genuine humility is saying, "God, on my own, I will never know you or understand you. I am blind, groping around a reality so much bigger than I am and so different from myself that I will never comprehend you unless you open my eyes and reveal yourself to me." Of course, that is exactly what God has done. He has revealed himself through his written word and then through the Word made flesh, Jesus, who came with grace and truth.

So, we can question each other's religious experiences, and we should question our own. Our experiences are never self-authenticating. They must be understood in the light of what Scripture teaches and has been tested by others in the body of Christ.

In our postmodern culture,
being nonjudgmental does not mean
respectfully disagreeing with another
person after considering his or her views.
No matter how they're spoken, words
that question another person's beliefs or
actions are considered judgmental.

## Being Nonjudgmental

The final New Absolute is the assertion that we must be nonjudgmental. People who know very little about Jesus feel certain they know one thing: Jesus never judged anyone, and neither should we.

Jesus did say, "Do not judge, or you too will be judged" (Matthew 7:1). But what did he mean by "do not judge"?

In our postmodern culture, being nonjudgmental does not mean respectfully disagreeing with another person after considering his or her views. No matter how they're spoken, words that question another person's beliefs or actions are considered judgmental. Even if you accept the person, you are considered hateful and even emotionally violent if you won't affirm his or her moral choices. The new mantra is "you're doing harm."

To understand what Jesus actually meant when he said, "Judge not," let's look at the words he spoke just a few verses later: "Do not give dogs what is sacred; do not throw your pearls to pigs. If you do, they may trample them under their feet, and turn and tear you to pieces" (Matthew 7:6). That's Jesus calling people dogs and swine, and he goes on to tell his followers to recognize them as such and to be careful around them. When you read *dogs* in verse 6, don't think of your little terrier bringing you your house slippers. These were wild street dogs. And when you read *pigs*, don't think of Babe or Arnold Ziffel on *Green Acres*. Jesus was referring to unclean, vicious animals that would attack and do great harm to people. He was telling his followers that there are people who are like wild dogs and vicious hogs. Give them what is holy, Jesus said, and they'll take it and use it to attack you and the Kingdom. So, don't give them that opportunity.

How nonjudgmental do these words of Jesus sound? Calling people dogs and swine—telling his followers to recognize these people for who they are—doesn't seem very tolerant, does it?

So, right after Jesus said, "Do not judge," he also told his followers to make some rather harsh judgments about some people. Either Jesus contradicted himself in the space of a few verses, or when he said, "Do not judge," he did not mean that we should embrace all behaviors and lifestyles.

The Greek verb used in Matthew 7:1—*krino*—means "to pronounce judgment" or "to condemn."[9] We are never to judge a person in the sense of condemning that person. We can disagree with an action—even condemn it as wrong—without condemning a person. It is God's prerogative to judge, not ours.

Writing about Jesus' prohibition of judging others, Friedrich Büchsel writes:

> [The saying] does not imply flabby indifference to the moral condition of others nor the blind renunciation of attempts at a true and serious appraisal of those with whom we have to live. What is unconditionally demanded is that such evaluations should be subject to the certainty that God's judgment falls also on those who judge, so that superiority, hardness and blindness to one's own faults are excluded and a readiness to forgive and to intercede is safeguarded.[10]

The most loving, truly accepting person who ever lived was also a harsh critic of injustice, hypocrisy, dishonesty, greed, sexual misbehavior, and false teaching. His love did not prevent him from telling people when their beliefs were wrong and their actions were sinful. You and I will never combine grace and truth as well as Jesus did. But that doesn't mean we shouldn't try. We should attempt to follow his example—humbly and with a primary concern about the log in our own eye—by striving to balance grace and truth as he did.

Perhaps because of the omnipresence of mass media, we are more aware than ever of the ugliness and damage created by persons who are intolerant, closed-minded, disparaging of others because of their faith, and judgmental. But the solution offered by postmodernism and the New Absolutes is a dead end. For the sake of tolerance, it tells us we must accept what God does not. In the name of being open, it states that we should make no distinctions between truth and falsehood. Championing pluralism, it encourages us to accept contradictory teachings about who God is and what it means to live a godly life. And with a misguided understanding of what it means to be nonjudgmental, it insists that we are failing to be Christlike if we make the same moral distinctions that Jesus made.

The fact that postmoderns who do not believe in absolute truth have created New Absolutes that all people are expected to live by tells us one thing: We human beings are looking for something or Someone to believe in who is greater than we are and who can give our lives meaning and significance. We can deny it with our heads, but our hearts yearn for something big enough to live for and solid enough to stand on. And those of us who know that the answer is a living relationship with the God of the universe through faith in Jesus Christ must not—out of fear or a need to be thought politically correct—keep the truth from a world that desperately needs to hear it. Love requires that we balance grace and truth.

# Reflect

o Do I generally hold my views with humility, acknowledging that I have much to learn? Am I open to learn from others whose experience of life is different from mine?

o How have I been influenced by the New Openness—the idea that we must accept all beliefs as equally valid?

o What is my understanding of tolerance? How does it compare to the culture's new definition of what it means to be tolerant?

o How have I been influenced by the three claims that pluralism would have us believe?

o How can I critique an action without condemning a person?

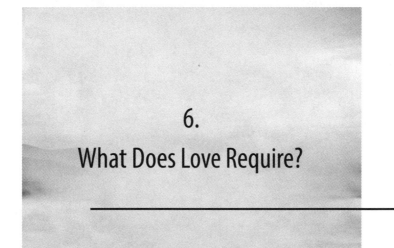

6.

# What Does Love Require?

# 6.
# What Does Love Require?

Jesus lived a "both-and" life, not an "either-or" life. Throughout his ministry we see him committed to both compassion for people and passion for truth. Rather than viewing grace and truth as being in opposition to each other and feeling the need to choose one or the other, Jesus believed and demonstrated that both are essential in representing the Father's heart and transforming the lives of people. And he told his disciples to follow his example.

"You are the salt of the earth," Jesus said. "But if the salt loses its saltiness, how can it be made salty again? It is no longer good for anything" (Matthew 5:13). Salt was important in the time of Jesus. It was used to season food—to bring out its best—and to preserve meat and fish from decaying and becoming rotten. Jesus tells us in this passage that people who follow him should be like salt, bringing out the best in others and keeping the good in this world from becoming spoiled and rotten.

The table salt we use in our homes is a combination of two elements: sodium and chlorine (NaCl). Sodium is never found alone in nature; it is always connected with another element. Its "gregarious" nature is evidenced by the fact that there are over 200 sodium compounds. You might say that it's willing to accept just about anything that's out there.

Chlorine, of course, is the gas that gives bleach its pungent odor. It's a powerful disinfectant, but you have to be careful with it. If misused, chlorine can be poisonous and destructive.

Grace is like sodium. Its nature is to reach out and receive. As long as grace is embracing people, it's similar to what we see in Jesus. But often in the name of grace, just about anything is accepted, including beliefs that contradict what the Scriptures reveal as the mind of God and behaviors that oppose his will.

Truth is more like chlorine. It's a cleansing agent, and there are times when we need to use it to "clean up" our thinking and the church's teachings. But by itself, truth can be offensive and difficult to be around—and if mishandled, truth even can be deadly.

If we're going to be salt, if we're going to make this world a better place as Jesus said we should, then we need to possess both grace and truth just as Jesus did. We must have compassion for people and passion for truth—not one instead of the other or one more than the other, but both together in equal measure.

I grew up in the late 1960s and early 70s. Conservative in theology, I was (and still am) liberal in heart. I learned at an early age from a fierce and enlightened mother that prejudice is wrong because everyone is made in the image of God. I attended an evangelical seminary situated in an idyllic New England town. I proudly wore my "Question Authority" pin on campus (which did not go over well), began a student group called Evangelicals for Social Action, and marched in Washington, DC against US involvement in El Salvador. After being there a year, I enrolled in the school's inner-city program during a time when angry white parents in parts of Boston were throwing bricks at buses carrying black children to schools in their neighborhood. My wife and I moved three blocks from where white housing met black. And the white kids in that neighborhood regularly sneered the world *liberal* at me as I walked by because I had told them that black children had a right to play in the same park where they played. Peggy and I attended a predominantly black church, and once when we had a black friend into our home, we were told that if we did that again, our house would be burned down. Instead, one afternoon Peggy came home to find that a dead cat had been smeared on our door.

I tell you this not to imply that we had it hard. We didn't. I tell you about my background because I want you to know that I don't want to be the one who fights for the rules. I want to be the one who exposes hypocrisy and makes certain that everyone is treated fairly. It's my heart to pull for the underdog and stand up for those who are mistreated and suffer discrimination. It's in my blood to challenge those in places of authority, especially if their policies harm or demean others. And yet I find myself championing the idea that there are rights and wrongs and absolute truths ("rules" you could call them) that apply to everyone. When the church and its leaders teach that we can disregard the moral teachings of the Bible because those teachings harm people, I feel a need to say, "Wait, it's not that easy. Truth matters, and we can't dismiss what God has revealed simply because it makes us uncomfortable or may offend others who don't agree with what the Scriptures teach." I defend "the rules," but doing so is not particularly comfortable for me. It's my nature to want to be the grace guy, not the truth guy.

Still, I know that I must be as passionate about the truth as I am about people because our faith is not either-or; it's both-and. Both-and is at the heart of the universe, and it's at the heart of the life and ministry of the One I love with all my heart and want to serve with all my life. I know that it takes truth and grace to be the salt of the earth and that if I choose either grace or truth instead of both, I am no longer fit to do ministry in the name of Jesus. If the church makes the gospel into "either grace or truth" instead of "both grace and truth," we will not be salt any longer and will not do the world any good.

I know that standing for the truth in a postmodern culture will bring criticism and charges of being narrow-minded and mean-spirited. It's common now for those of us who promote an orthodox Christian faith and uphold moral and spiritual truths that Christians have held for two thousand years to be pummeled as unloving. Our words, we are told, do harm. Our views are considered exclusionary and non-Christlike. And we, as persons, are thought to be uncharitable and condemning.

My colleagues and I who work in our denomination to maintain a traditional, biblical view of sexuality and marriage are often criticized in print or in person as being cold-hearted, judgmental, self-righteous, and outright mean. It always amazes me when those who are so adamant about being non-judgmental can condemn with the broadest of strokes those with whom they disagree and have never met. The charge beneath all the name-calling is that God is love and that our views and our actions are far from loving.

Such comments make we wonder about the words we use. I'm convinced that part of the problem we have in discussing our differences could be that we have different meanings for the word *love*. What does it mean to love someone? How we answer that question is, to a large degree, determined by our definition of *love*.

I facilitate a course at our church called "How to Love and Help Your Adult Child." Parents who attend are concerned about their adult children (who are anywhere from twenty to fifty years old). Some of their children are alcoholic, some are

If the church makes the gospel into
"either grace or truth" instead of
"both grace and truth,"
we will not be salt any longer and
will not do the world any good.

guilty of criminal behavior, some are bipolar, some are unable to hold a job, and some move from one unhealthy emotional relationship to another. When the parents arrive for the first class, the room is filled with fear and sadness and pain—and love. All of the parents who attend, no matter how much they have suffered as a result of a child's choices, still love their child.

The question we wrestle with throughout the course is this: *What does it mean to love a child who is making poor decisions?* Some parents, even if they have no belief that their child will ever stop drugging or drinking, want to give their child money and shelter so that he or she will be safe. They are certain that is what love would do. They say that they love their child too much to let him or her be on the streets, cold and hungry and vulnerable to harm.

But there are other parents in the same room who are convinced that love requires a different response. They believe that the most caring approach they can take is to allow their child to live with the consequences of his or her choices, even if it means living on the streets. It's not easy not knowing where your child is; not knowing if she is safe; not knowing if he is hungry or high or hurt. It's not easy to let your child wander off to a far country like the father in the story of the prodigal son, especially when you know that he or she might be glad to come home (as long as a change in behavior isn't required) if only you asked. It's hell hearing the phone ring and rushing to answer, hoping it's your child saying that he has changed but fearing that it might be the sheriff telling you that your child is dead. But these parents, believing that their child will never make healthy choices as long as they make it easy for him or her to be unhealthy, have determined that love requires them to do something that is very painful—both for them and for their child. And that is to say, "We love you. We accept you. But you can't come home until you want to change your life."

Both sets of parents care deeply for their child. Neither loves their child more than the other. But the words they speak to their children are often very different, as are the actions they take.

I think in some ways that's where the church is. Progressives and traditionalists both love people who are hurting and struggling and may be making wrong choices. We can differ on how best to help without needing to label those who disagree with us as unloving, cold-hearted, or mean-spirited. I wouldn't allow such name calling to occur in the class at my church, and I hope we won't allow it in our debates about what love requires as we try to help persons who are in need of God's grace and truth. What we need most is not a discussion that attacks each other's motives but a dialogue that helps us understand what love is and what it requires from us as followers of Jesus.

So, back to the question: What does love require of us? Does loving others mean that we must celebrate their lifestyle? Does caring for another person mean we must accept and support every choice he or she makes? If so, then surely Jesus was not a loving person. As we've seen, Jesus told people— all people—to repent of their wrong choices and sin no more— in other words, to change their "lifestyle." Jesus told the greedy, the self-righteous, the sexually immoral, and those who taught falsehood as truth to repent—not because he did not love them but because he did.

There was no iceberg in the heart of Jesus, no emptiness of compassion in his soul; there was only the purest love the world has ever known. And yet for Jesus, loving and serving others did not mean accepting everything they did or everything they taught. It meant caring enough to tell people the truth they needed to hear—the truth that would set them free.

M. Scott Peck defined love this way: "the will to extend one's self for the purpose of nurturing . . . another's spiritual

Jesus told the greedy,
the self-righteous, the sexually immoral,
and those who taught falsehood as
truth to repent—not because he did not
love them but because he did.

growth."[1] I don't deny—in fact, I decry—the fact that there are some conservative Christians who use demeaning language toward persons with same-sex attraction and who find it difficult to feel compassion for or have friendships with persons who are gay. That's not who I am, and it's not any orthodox church leader I have known personally. But I know there are some conservative Christians who are unwilling to "extend" themselves to love, accept, and serve all persons as they are. And out of love let me say that they need to repent and let the compassion of Christ change their hearts. We who claim to follow Jesus must protect those who are attacked and disparaged whatever the reason. We must welcome those who are rejected whatever the cause. We must walk with those who are a work in progress because we all are.

There is also a word of caution in Dr. Peck's definition of love for progressives, and it is that we must think carefully about what it means to nurture another person's spiritual growth. Is spiritual growth nothing more than learning to accept one's self, or is it a process of transformation from who we are into the persons God wants us to be? Is spiritual growth ignoring some of the teachings of the New Testament in order to affirm "the new thing" that progressives claim the Spirit is now doing, or is it learning the truths of the Bible and living accordingly? Is spiritual growth coming to a place where we believe we know the motives of others and judge them for having cold hearts and being self-righteous and prideful, or is it believing that we can have real differences on important issues—and even write about them—without impugning each other's motives?

Progressives tell us that the way of Christ is the way of love, and I agree. But what we don't find in Jesus is the love of the sentimentalist. What we don't witness in the ministry of Jesus is grace without truth. And what we don't see in Jesus is a compassion that accepts people without also telling them,

"Now, go and sin no more." Jesus extended himself to nurture the spiritual growth of people, and that always meant speaking to people not only about the Father's love but also about their brokenness and sin—and then teaching them about and loving them into a new way of life.

A good friend accepts you, believes in you, and encourages you. And if this person is truly a good friend, he or she also tells you when you are failing. Our best friends are the ones who love us enough to be honest with us and even hurt our feelings if that's what it takes for us to make better choices and to become healthy. In Proverbs we read, "Wounds from a friend can be trusted" (Proverbs 27:6). A good friend isn't the one who only makes us feel good about who we are but the one who also loves us enough to help us become better than we are spiritually and emotionally—and sometimes that means speaking words that are difficult for our friend to say and for us to hear. But sometimes that's what love requires.

I hope that we—as individual Christians and as the church— will be a good friend to all—the greedy, the self-righteous, the sexually immoral, the prejudiced, the alcoholic, and the judgmental, to name a few. Being a good friend means loving people as they are, speaking the truth they need to hear, and then nurturing their growth so that they can become the persons God desires them to be. Anything less and we will fail God and the people we are called to help. We must be committed to being a good friend to people who need to know the hope that is to be found in Jesus Christ. And that means combining grace and truth the way that Jesus did—both-and, not either-or.

Before writing these final paragraphs, I again watched the video of Nik Wallenda making his way across a tightrope 1,500 feet above the canyon floor—with the wind blowing strongly and he struggling to keep his balance and stay on the wire for an excruciating twenty-two minutes. Funny, I knew he made it, but my stomach tightened and my heart started racing all over again. It just looks so incredibly difficult and dangerous. One minute he had to lean his pole a little more to one side to stay on the wire, and then in the next minute he had to lean it more in the other direction to keep his balance. But he did it, and the world watched in awe.

There will be times when we will have to lean toward grace and other times when we will have to emphasize truth. As we talk with and minister to wounded persons, especially those who have been hurt by the church, it will be right for us to favor the side of grace. As the winds of our culture blow in the direction of postmodernism and moral relativism, we will have to lean a little harder in the direction of truth. It's a balancing act, and there's freedom—actually a necessity—to favor one side of the pole and then the other. But all of the time we must keep a firm grip on both sides, knowing that if we let go of either, the results will be tragic.

There's something else Nik Wallenda did as he made his journey across the canyon. Over and over again he called out to Jesus. One of the bravest men in the world, Wallenda was humble enough to ask Jesus to help him stay on the wire and keep his balance.

You and I are called to something that is terribly difficult and immensely important. And if we get it wrong, the results will be disastrous. We are called through our words and our actions to make known the One who was a friend of sinners and the transformer of lives. If we choose either grace or truth, we won't keep our balance or represent him well. It's only when we combine both compassion for people and a passion for truth that we will walk in his footsteps and be used by him to do the work of his Kingdom. And there's nothing more essential for us to do than humble ourselves, confess our need for help, and call out to Jesus for strength and wisdom.

# Reflect

o What does it mean to love someone who is making poor decisions? How can I show love and care without supporting every choice he or she makes?

o How can I share the truth someone needs to hear without being perceived as unloving, cold-hearted, or mean-spirited?

o Am I willing to protect those who are attacked and disparaged whatever the reason? Am I willing to welcome those who are rejected whatever the cause? Am I willing to walk with those who are a work in progress, recognizing that I am too?

o How can I discuss important issues without impugning others' motives?

o What does it mean to be a good friend to all?

o Am I relying on Jesus' help as I seek to balance grace and truth?

# Notes

## Introduction

1. "The truth is out there" is a phrase popularized by the television show *The X Files*. http://en.Wikipedia.org/wiki/The_X-Files.

## Chapter 1

1. http://www.cbsnews.com/news/nik-wallenda-completes-tightrope-walk-across-gorge-near-grand-canyon/.

## Chapter 2

1. Francis Schaeffer, *The God Who Is There* (London: Hodder and Stoughton Limited, 1968), 36.
2. Richard J. Needham, "Speak the Truth," cited in *Quotable Quotes* (Pleasantville, NY: Reader's Digest, 1997), 157.
3. Theodore Roosevelt, https://sites.google.com/site/byuheroesofhistory/theodoreroosevelt.
4. "Splagchnizomai," *Strong's Concordance*, http://biblesuite.com/greek/4697.htm.
5. Herbert Agar, "A Time for Greatness," (1942): cited in *Oxford Dictionary of Quations by Subject*, ed. Susan Ratcliffe, 2nd ed. (New York: Oxford University Press Inc., 2010), 486.
6. T. S.Eliot, "Burnt Norton," in *Four Quartets*, (New York: A Harvest Book/Harcourt, Inc., 1968), 14; http://www.coldbacon.com/poems/fq.html.

7. Fyodor Dostoyevsky, *The Brothers Karamazov* (New York: Bantam Dell, 1970), 55.

8. James Allen, *Above Life's Turmoil* (1910; reprint, Rockville, MD: Wildside Press, 2010), 31.

9. A. W. Tozer, *The Knowledge of the Holy* (New York: HarperCollins, 1961), 1.

10. "Who is God?" *Life* Magazine, December 1990, 47-86.

11. John Donne, "Meditation XVII," *Devotions Upon Emergent Occasions and Death's Duel* (New York: Vintage Books, 1999), 1-3.

12. Ibid.

13. Ibid.

14. "Harmartia," *Strong's Concordance*, http:// biblesuite.com/greek/266.htm.

15. American Psychological Association, "Answers to Your Questions For a Better Understanding of Sexual Orientation and Homosexuality," http://www.apa.org/topics/lgbt/orientation.aspx?item=4.

16. Os Guinness, *Time for Truth* (Grand Rapids: Baker Books, 2000), 10-11.

17. Alexander Solzhenitsyn, "Nobel Lecture, 1970," http://www.nobelprize.org/nobel_prizes/literature/laureates/1970/solzhenitsyn-lecture.html.

## Chapter 3

1. C. S. Lewis, *Reflections on the Psalms* (New York: A Harvest Book/Harcourt, Inc., 1958/1986), 62.

2. Protagaras, http://dictionary.reference.com/browse/man+is+the+measure+of+all+things.

3. Richard Dawkins, *The God Delusion* (New York: Houghton Mifflin Company, 2006), 5.

4. Richard Dawkins, "Is Science a Religion?" in *The Humanist*, January/February 1997.

5. Richard Dawkins, "The Flying Spaghetti Monster," October 13, 2006, http://www.salon.com/2006/10/13/dawkins_3/.

6. John Templeton, *Possibilities for Over One Hundredfold More Spiritual Information: The Humble Approach in Theology and Science* (Templeton Foundation Press, 2000), quoted in "Philanthropic Vision," http://www.templeton.org/sir-john-templeton/philanthropic-vision.

7. Richard Dawkins, *River Out of Eden: A Darwinian View of Life* (New York: Basic Books, 1995), 133.

8. C. S. Lewis, *Mere Christianity* (New York: HarperSanFrancisco, 2001), 136-37.

9. Thomas V. Morris, *Making Sense of It All: Pascal and the Meaning of Life* (Grand Rapids, MI: Wm. B. Eerdmans, 1992), 130.

10. Kahlil Gibran, *The Prophet,* Suheil Bushrui, editor (London: Oneworld Publications, 2012), 55.

11. G. K. Chesterton, *Orthodoxy* (Colorado Springs: Waterbrook Press, 2001), 38-39.

## Chapter 4

1. Allan Bloom, *The Closing of the American Mind* (New York: Simon and Schuster, 1987), 25.

2. William Shakespeare, *Measure for Measure,* Act V, Scene I.

3. Gary Nicholson, "The Trouble with the Truth," © Four Sons Music, Sony/ATV Cross Keys Publishing, Song/ATV Tree Publishing.

## Chapter 5

1. Allan Bloom, *The Closing of the American Mind* (New York: Simon and Schuster, 1987), 26.

2. G. K. Chesterton, *Autobiography*, in *Collected Works, Vol. 16* (San Francisco: Ignatius Press, 1988), 212.

3. Bloom, 38.

4. "Swaggart apologizes for talk of killing gays," NBC News.com, September 23, 2004, http://www.nbcnews.com/id/6074380/#.UpD_dyg_4Q8.

5. Evelyn Beatrice Hall, *The Friends of Voltaire* (London: Smith, Elder & Co., 1906 [facsimile]), 199, http://www.reference.com/motif/society/i-disapprove-of-what-you-say-but-i-will-defend-to-the-death-your-right-to-say-it.

6. N. T. Wright, Youtube video, "The Bible on Slavery, Sexism and Homosexuality," http://www.youtube.com/watch?v=2HTT64AqigM.

7. C. S. Lewis from the essay "Man or Rabbit?" in *God in the Dock* (Grand Rapids, MI: Wm. B. Eerdmans Publishing, 1972), 108-109.

8. "The Blind Men and the Elephant," http://www.constitution.org/col/blind_men.htm.

9. "Krino," *The New American Standard New Testament Greek Lexicon*, http://www.biblestudytools.com/lexicons/greek/nas/krino.html.

10. Friedrich Büchsel, *Theological Dictionary of the New Testament,* Vol. 3, Gerhard Kittel, ed. (Grand Rapids, MI: Wm. B. Eerdmans Publishing Company, 1965, 1979), 939.

## Chapter 6

1. M. Scott Peck, *The Road Less Traveled* (New York: Simon and Schuster, 1978), 81.